DISCARDED

# GEORGE WASHINGTON

AND OTHER

## AMERICAN ADDRESSES

↑ 806989

# GEORGE WASHINGTON

### AND OTHER

### AMERICAN ADDRESSES

BY

FREDERIC HARRISON

LIBRARY OF
LAMAR STATE COLLEGE OF TECHNOLOGY

*Essay Index Reprint Series*

 BOOKS FOR LIBRARIES PRESS
FREEPORT, NEW YORK

First Published 1901
Reprinted 1969

STANDARD BOOK NUMBER:
8369-1263-2

LIBRARY OF CONGRESS CATALOG CARD NUMBER:
71-86758

PRINTED IN THE UNITED STATES OF AMERICA

*I am permitted to Inscribe*

*This Volume of Addresses given in the United States*

*to*

*His Excellency*

THE HON. JOSEPH H. CHOATE

Litt.D.

*American Ambassador in London*

# NOTE

The following Addresses were given in February and March, 1901, at various Societies and Universities of the United States. The occasion of my visit was an invitation with which I was honoured by the Union League Club of Chicago to deliver the public Address in the Auditorium of that city, on the annual commemoration of the birthday of George Washington. My thanks are due to the American Ambassador in London, who transmitted to me from his friends there this and similar invitations from various Universities, and who adds to his kindness by permitting me to inscribe his name on this volume.

The first two addresses were in substance published in the annual Report of the celebration by the Union League Club of Chicago. The Lecture on the Writings of King Alfred was published separately in May last. The other Addresses have not previously been printed.

# CONTENTS

|      |                                           | PAGE |
|------|-------------------------------------------|------|
| I.   | George Washington and the Republican Ideal | 3    |
| II.  | Abraham Lincoln                           | 31   |
| III. | The Millenary of King Alfred              | 41   |
| IV.  | The Writings of King Alfred               | 71   |
| V.   | The Dutch Republic                        | 105  |
| VI.  | Recent Biographies of Cromwell            | 141  |
| VII. | Republicanism and Democracy               | 165  |
| VIII.| Personal Reminiscences                    | 191  |
| IX.  | Municipal Government                      | 219  |
| X.   | The Nineteenth Century                    | 237  |

# GEORGE WASHINGTON AND THE
REPUBLICAN IDEAL

# George Washington and the Republican Ideal

ADDRESS IN THE AUDITORIUM, CHICAGO, FEBRUARY 22, 1901

WE meet on a day which for more than a century has been held sacred by the men of this vast Continent — the day which ever increasing millions who speak our common tongue will celebrate for centuries to come, and hand down from generation to generation as a national heirloom and trust. The colossal Republic of the West had a Founder around whose name gather memories more real and solid than those which enshrined the half-mythical founders of republics in antiquity; whilst in valour, sagacity, and nobility of nature, George Washington was the peer of the most splendid heroes of the ancient or the modern world.

The historian has too often to confess that the statesmen of modern times have seldom presented to us types of that romantic heroism, of the chivalry, the purity of soul, the sublime surrender of self, which we ascribe to a Leonidas, a Marcus Aurelius, a King Alfred, or a Godfrey de Bouillon. Too many of the chiefs who have made or saved a nation have been stained by faithlessness, cunning, ambition, cruelty, and vice. It is consoling to think — it gives us fresh hopes of humanity to know — that the latest in the roll of the creators of nations has a spotless record of honour as a man, as a soldier, as a statesman;

> "Whatever record leap to light,
> He never shall be shamed —"

Whilst his memory is revered by the civilised world in Europe, it is nowhere held in such personal affection as with the people whom he defeated and whose dominion he shook off; for all right-minded Englishmen now feel that his work was a real gain — albeit a bitter lesson — to our own nation; whilst his noble character and unsullied career as soldier, as statesman, as patriot, add new glory to our common race. George Washington is as much one of our great English heroes as Alfred the Great or Shakespeare is one of yours. The robust nature, the ancestral speech, are the common prerogatives of our blood. And as the wildest dreamer in Great Britain cannot conceive our two peoples being other than independent nations to-day, we have nothing but honour for the hero who achieved the happy and inevitable separation.

I am well aware that since, on American soil, the memory of Washington has been celebrated for more than a century by tens of thousands of eloquent tongues, I ought now to pass to some more general theme, and not presume to add my mite to the vast monument which ages of impassioned oratory have raised to perpetuate his name. The great historian of Athens said in one of his pregnant phrases: "Illustrious men have the whole earth for their tomb." How true is it that the whole American Continent is the tomb of Washington; for from the Atlantic to the Pacific, from the Gulf of Mexico to Behring's Straits, every inch of soil bears witness to his life, and is made sacred by his immortal presence.

In the most memorable of all memorial orations, the great Athenian chief said: "— no need for prolix panegyrics amongst men who know it all so well." And I feel that it is almost presumption in a visitor to speak to American citizens of the Founder of their Republic. But since you have done this honour to myself — and indeed to my country — in inviting an Englishman to speak to you of Washington, it seems to be fitting that I should tell you how he looks to English eyes, how deeply his memory is cherished in the old country of his ancestors — and of your ancestors.

I shall say to you nothing that I should not say to my own countrymen — nothing indeed that I have not often said to my own countrymen. Twice before, in our own Hall in London, I have given addresses in the Centennial Commemoration of Washington that we held in recent years, and I will say now nothing which I did not say then. That name is so great and wide that there shall be no exclusive monopoly in it. It cannot be limited to his State of Virginia — it cannot be limited to the Old States of the Union —

it cannot be limited to America itself. It belongs to the Anglo-Saxon race. It belongs in fine to Humanity at large.

Nor am I about to insult a noble memory by idle panegyric or extravagant words. Of all great men in history George Washington is he whom it would be most unseemly to flatter or to canonise. He, who was the soul of scrupulous moderation and sterling veracity, should teach us to treat him in that same spirit of self-control and truth. As the English historian of the Georgian era has said : " It was the transparent integrity of the character of Washington " which enabled him, soldier as he was, to found a democratic republic with no shadow on it of military despotism. It is in the spirit of aiming at transparent integrity that I shall seek to speak of him. I shall not presume to speak of him as he appears to American eyes. I will try to say what he seems to our English eyes. And perhaps the cool and independent judgment of those who cannot claim to be fellow-citizens of his, and who were once his enemies, may more accord with the unobtrusive genius of the great republican chief than that unbounded adulation in which for a hundred years he has been addressed and canonised here.

The eminent historian of the Eighteenth Century whom I have quoted tells us this : —

" Of all the great men in history he was the most invariably judicious, and there is scarcely a rash word or action or judgment recorded of him. No act of his public life can be traced to personal caprice, ambition, or resentment. In the despondency of long-continued failure, in the elation of sudden success, at times when his soldiers were deserting by hundreds, and when malignant plots were formed against his reputation, amid the constant quarrels, rivalries, and jealousies of his subordinates, in the dark hour of national ingratitude, and in the most universal and intoxicating flattery, he was always the same calm, wise, just, and single-minded man, pursuing the course which he believed to be right without fear or favour or fanaticism; equally free from the passions which spring from interest and from the passions that spring from imagination. He was in the highest sense of the word a gentleman and a man of honour, and he carried into public life the severest standard of private morals. There is scarcely another instance in history of such a man having reached and maintained the highest position in the convulsions of civil war and of a great popular agitation."

In England we are accustomed to draw parallels between the career — though not the character — of George Washington and that of our great Protector, Oliver Cromwell, and of the Founder of the Dutch Commonwealth, William the Silent, Prince of Orange. All three carried on in mature life a long and desperate struggle in a fierce civil war against the tyranny of a retrograde king. All three, after beating back the armies of the tyrant, were chosen by their people to be the first chiefs of a new Commonwealth. And all three showed an organising genius of the first order in welding into a nation the broken sections of the people whom they had saved from slavery by their arms.

But the parallel between William the Silent and George Washington is peculiarly close. These two in a special sense created new nations. Their work subsists to-day after more than three centuries in the first case, and more than a century in the other case. The direct and immediate work of Cromwell was quickly undone. His indirect and permanent work has to be traced in a number of obscure and gradual effects. Oliver deeply modified the history of an old nation: he did not create a new nation.

The analogies of William the Silent and Washington lie in this. Each was the soul of an obstinate contest to secure self-government against a foreign monarchy. Both were men of birth and wealth, conservative in spirit, old servants and soldiers of the foreign sovereign. Both had to face defeat, disappointment, jealousies, discord, treachery and panic. Both, when raised to supreme power, showed splendid public spirit and devotion to their cause, and genius as statesmen even higher than their ability in war. The people whom they led to freedom were not so unequal in number. But, whereas the nation which the Prince founded remains after three centuries no larger in area or in population than of old, the nation which Washington created is amongst the greatest on earth — with boundless possibilities of development.

On the other hand, in a grand point of character, Washington will ever stand out in history as greater than William — greater than almost any statesman in supreme place in the whole record of the modern world. His unshaken devotion to right, his perfect justice, his transparent truthfulness and lofty sense of honour, will ever place him above even the best of modern statesmen in virtue. That which sets him in a rank by himself among chiefs of state is the unfailing honour and guileless candour of his whole public career, toward both home and foreign opponents. Compare the diplomacy or the policy of Washington with that of Frederic the Great, or Richelieu, or Peter the Great, or Louis XI, or Elizabeth of England, William of Orange, or Oliver Cromwell — we find Washington to be ever what the Greek philosopher dreamed of, but never found in the flesh — "The man who stood four-square, upright, without reproach." It makes one more hopeful of the future and less despondent of the present, to know that, even in these later ages, there has been found a chief such that, in a desperate rebellion and the birth-throes of a new commonwealth, with treachery, intrigue and mendacity around him, tempting him to meet craft with craft, violence and injustice with fraud — "the fierce light that beats upon" the seat of a President as it does on a monarch's throne, can reveal no falsehood, no baseness, no outrage, no crime.

I quoted a couplet from Tennyson's grand ode on the burial of our Duke of Wellington; and I cannot help feeling how well many of these noble lines serve to describe Washington — some of them indeed more justly even than Wellington.

Listen to these: —

> "O friends, our chief state-oracle is mute :
> The statesman-warrior, moderate, resolute,
> Whole in himself, a common good.
> Mourn for the man of amplest influence,
> Yet clearest of ambitious crime —
> Great in council and great in war,
> Foremost captain of his time,
> Rich in saving common-sense
> And, as the greatest only are,
> In his simplicity, sublime — "

Are not these words as true of Washington as of Wellington — nay, perhaps when applied to Washington, less marked by exaggeration or pride?

We often think of Washington in connection with our own Oliver Cromwell. Both came of old and honourable English families, and it is odd that it was the protectorate of Oliver which drove the great-grandfather of Washington, a zealous royalist, to found a new family in Virginia. Both Washington and Cromwell were the eldest sons of the junior branch of ancient and wealthy landowners. Both had only elementary schooling. Both were summoned before they were of age to protect a family of orphans; both were in close alliance with the gallant family of Fairfax. Both were called after passing middle life to direct an obstinate civil war and then to govern and organise a broken and distracted nation.

In this matter the task of Washington was in one sense greater than that of Cromwell. England at the close of the civil war was still an organic whole; and in the army of the Ironsides it had an overwhelming and solid force of disciplined enthusiasts, such as the world has but rarely seen. Washington's task as a soldier had been to organise into an army a floating body of raw volunteers, each of whom thought himself the equal of every other citizen whatsoever, and to wring from local and jealous committees the essential supplies and funds.

His career as a statesman was of even grander order. In his eight years' tenure of supreme power in the new nation, he had a great and peculiar task in which he amply succeeded. He was called not merely to preside over a nation, to administer a government — but to make a nation — to create a government. He found nothing but the raw material of a nation and a government. He left these materials an organic body, able to live and grow. From the first, there appeared that antithesis between the central and the local interests which in my memory has plunged the United States into a tremendous conflict, and in other forms leaves problems yet for final solution. The conduct of Washington in this antinomy of ideas was a perfect model of wisdom and self-control. He himself, as a man saturated with conservative and governing instincts, inclined to the principle of a strong central authority. At the same time he saw the deep bias of the American people toward a local patriotism, the development of the physical and social peculiarities of the vast American Continent, and the need for extreme moderation for the powers to be conferred on any central executive.

The consummate sagacity and dominant virtue of Washington united the two parties and saved the young commonwealth from a premature explosion of the struggle which began sixty years after his death. His second Presidency was more harassing and critical even than his first. But his power to ride the storm — to impress his spirit upon the nation — not by force, not by eloquence, not by logic, but by the apostolic power of a faultless character for rectitude, self-devotion and wisdom — this, I say, forms one of the great moral laws graven on the imperishable decalogue of history, one of the consoling truths which cheer us in the task as we groan over those weary annals of the madness of nations and the ambition of statesmen. When the restlessness of factions sought to flourish the Stars and Stripes in the face of all comers, Washington upheld the banner he had formed as the emblem of neutrality, peace, consolidation, and financial probity. In making these ideas the mottoes of the commonwealth, George Washington founded the indissoluble union of an organic, industrial law-abiding nation, with a boundless power of expansion and a paradise of prosperity before it, and conferred on his fellow-citizens a service greater, nobler and more far-reaching than when he led them to victory against a foreign tyrant.

And the close of such a career was in all things worthy of its spotless record. To compel his fellow-citizens to suffer him to descend from what was a seat of power far above the throne of monarchs, to do this in the maturity of his physical and mental powers, and solely as a great example to his successors, has given the world a new conception of moral dignity and republican simplicity. It was no case of a dictator who, as the poet says, " stalked in savage grandeur home " : — it was no Charles V seeking refuge in a convent from disease and disappointment. It was the one abdication of power in recorded history that was based on public duty and not on personal motive. And now the capital city of this vast republic bears his name; and his home and burial place are become the place of pilgrimage to the civilised world; so that he lies enshrined in the central pulse and brain of the nation he created, his spirit, we imagine, brooding over the council-boards of his successors : —

> " And so sepulchred in such pomp doth lie,
> That Kings for such a tomb would wish to die."

The Roman historian left this famous phrase of one of his characters — felix opportunitate mortis. How much more true is this of George Washington if we paraphrase it to mean — blest in all the circumstances of his end! This came by a quick and easy stroke as he approached three-score and ten at the height of his reputation and authority, with the prosperous future of his country assured. How few of the heroes and creators of nations lived to see even the first fruits of the work of their lives! How few have passed through a career beset with temptations, perils, and dilemmas, without once giving way to a single act of folly, one deed of injustice, meanness, or passion! It is the unique privilege of Washington that he lived to see the crown of his work, and left it to his country as a stainless record.

It is a rare fortune when the hero can close his eyes with the confident hope that he has not lived in vain, with no crushing remorse that his memory will descend with a burden of offence to generations unborn. Heroes too often die in the midst of visible disaster, in agony, in humiliation — and if such great souls could ever lose hope, we might almost say in despair. Too often their dying eyes are darkened with gloom and gathering storms. These Christs of Humanity for the most part die upon their cross, unconscious of the future worth of their lives and of the distant issues which were destined to spring out of their sacrifice. We who to-day so crave after visible success, who are so prone to measure every life by its practical result in the present, who scorn the labours which are not cheered by the shouts of the mob, with fame, with conquests, with gold, let us remember that the heroes to whom nations owe all they prize have seldom any crown of glory to dazzle their dying eyes, and too often lay down their weary heads beneath a crown of thorns. Too often they expire with the cruel cry within their hearts, if not upon their lips — Eli! Eli! lama sabacthani! — My God! My God! why hast thou forsaken me?

From this last agony of soul George Washington

was free, as he assuredly was free from any ground for remorse. But he could little have conceived that, within one hundred years, his people would have increased some twenty-fold, or that this great city would be standing on ground which was then an Indian wilderness.

There is a profound moral in the life of George Washington and his place in the world's history. Here is a simple citizen, by birth a quiet country gentleman, who wins triumphant success in one of the most memorable of modern wars, and welds into a nation a scattered body of colonists, so that within a hundred years they are grown to be one of the biggest, richest, most progressive people that ever existed on this earth. He himself is an object of veneration to more than a hundred millions who are of his race and language — even though a third of them are of the people he repulsed — for all who speak our common tongue regard him as one of the noblest figures in the annals of their race. And yet, he is no Alexander or Cæsar, no Charlemagne or Napoleon. He was no born soldier; he made himself a warrior by dint of an indomitable nature. Nor was he a dictator, such an one as mankind bow down to as more than man. And yet, does history record any result of work so rapid, so colossal, so multifarious?

The grand endowment of Washington was character, not imagination; judgment, not subtlety; not brilliancy, but wisdom. The wisdom of Washington was the genius of common-sense, glorified into unerring truth of view. He had that true courage, physical and moral, that purity of soul, that cool judgment which is bred in the bone of the English-speaking race. But in Washington these qualities, not rare on either side of the Atlantic, were developed to a supreme degree and were found in absolute perfection. He thus became the transfiguration of the stalwart, just, truthful, prudent citizen, having that essence of good sense which amounts to true genius, that perfection of courage which is true heroism, that transparent unselfishness which seems to us the special mark of the saint.

The American commonwealth was made by the halo of virtue, honour, and truthfulness which seemed to radiate from the very soul of its first President. May it long continue to guide the destinies of the republic! It is character that makes heroes, more than any genius. It is character which creates nations, more than imagination. It is character round which nations rally when the stress comes on them, and confusion looms in their midst. It is character, unselfishness, honesty, and truth which in the long run rule the world and determine its destinies sooner or later. It may be often obscured, and may be long ere it is fully revealed. But the foremost apostle of this sacred gospel of noble character in these modern ages was the founder of the United States, who was indeed a star on high of the first magnitude in all that constitutes a grand and imposing nature.

I pass on to say a few words on that republican

ideal, of which George Washington furnishes the eternal type. When I utter the phrase republican ideal there comes into my mind the memory of that wonderful picture of it in the noblest of all speeches as recorded by the greatest of all historians — the Funeral Oration of Pericles in Thucydides.

"The republican government," he says, "is one that feels no jealousy or rivalry with the institutions of others. We have no wish to imitate them; we prefer to be an example to them. It is true that our constitution is a democracy, for it is framed in the interest of all, not of any privileged class. Yet, whilst the law secures to all in their private claims equal justice without favour of persons, we still recognise the value of personal superiority, when a citizen is in any way distinguished by his attainments; and he is raised to eminence in the public service, not as a matter of privilege, but as the prize of his merits. Nor again is poverty a bar with us, to hinder a citizen who can confer some service on the state. Public office is a career open to great capacity, however humble may be the station in which it is found. Public life is with our people absolutely free to all. In our private life we are not suspicious of each other, nor do we quarrel with a citizen who chooses to live his own life just as it pleases himself. But whilst ours is the land of perfect liberty to each citizen to live freely as it suits him, we are bound by loyalty to the common law which we reverence as the voice of the republic. We obey only the law which is ordained to protect every man from wrong doing. And we respect the unwritten law of public opinion which visits those who transgress the moral code with the reprobation of their fellow-citizens.

"Nor do we forget to provide relaxations after the urgent labour of our lives. We hold regular festivals and solemn thanksgivings on the appointed days throughout the year. In our homes our mode of life is cheerful so that we banish all sense of gloom. The vastness of our republic affords us all the fruits and resources of the entire earth, of which all the goods that it affords flow freely in to us, and we enjoy the products of other lands as easily as those of our own land. Our state is open to the world and is the resort of men from other countries. We welcome the foreigner who comes to us, and leave him free to inspect all we have to show him and to profit by all that we can teach him. We rely not on cunning devices and secret intrigues, but we trust our own right arms, our own stout hearts. We are not ground down by a conscription, which makes every citizen a compulsory soldier; yet, when the call of our country comes, we can show a front as brave as any, and we prove to them that the volunteer citizen in arms is at least the match of the conscript who is forced to pass his youth in the barrack.

"As men, we love all things that are beautiful, yet our taste is for the simple and plain. We delight in mental culture, but it does not make us the weaker in action. Wealth we use for practical ends of a real kind, not to boast of or to display to the world. It is no disgrace to a citizen to avow that he is a poor man; the true disgrace is to be too idle to earn his own living. Our citizens do not neglect the affairs of the republic, because they are absorbed in the affairs of their own household and fortune. And those who are occupied with their private business find time to take a very active part in politics. It is our way that the citizen who is utterly indifferent to public affairs is looked on as a drone. It is not for every citizen to take the lead in dictating a policy; but he is bound to be a sound judge of the policy submitted to his acceptance. We count the true mischief in public policy to lie, not in effective discussion of the platforms before the nation, but rather in adopting a policy without that knowledge of the facts which serious discussion would impart. The gift of our people is to be able to look all round a problem before we take it up in action, and then to act when reflection has done its work. Whereas we know there are people who rush into difficulties with the heedlessness of ignorance, and then, when they begin to understand all it means, entirely lose heart.

"To sum it all up together, we may boast that our commonwealth is the school of the civilised world. Each citizen of our republic is endowed with the power in his own person of adapting himself to the most varied form of activity and life with consummate versatility and ease. This is no passing and idle word, but truth and fact; the proof of which lies in the splendid position which our republic now holds in the world to-day. There is a latent strength within us, which ever rises above even all that our neighbours expect that we can show. The enemies whom we overcome on the battle-field submit to be defeated by a power so great; and those who have to bear our empire admit that their master is worthy to bear rule. Of this there are ample witnesses, in those mighty monuments of our power which will make us the wonder of this age and ages to come. It needs no rhetoric to prove it. Every land and every sea bears witness to our energy and our valour, and on every soil we have planted eternal memorials of the good we can do to our friends and the harm we could inflict upon our foes."

Such is the type of the republic painted by the great statesman of Athens at the zenith of her glory.

How far it is reproduced — how far it can be reproduced in our age, it is not for me to say. There are some features in the picture which are essential elements of the true republic. The essence of a republic is a state where power is reserved not to privilege but to merit, where it is exercised in the sole interest of the community, and never in the interest of any class or order. In the true republic all authority is a trust committed by the commonwealth to those who are held capable of using it best in the common service of all. Nothing hereditary can remain in it. Birth cannot create any privilege, any priority in honour, power, or right of any kind. And as in the true republic there is no privilege for birth, so neither is there any privilege for wealth. The service of the state, even in its highest post, must be freely open to every citizen, whatever his birth, his breeding, or his means, provided only he be capable to fill it. There is no title to any public office but personal worthiness alone; there is no lawful object of public activity, but the common interest of the community at large.

There are three tests of the true republic — (1) that power rests on fitness to rule; (2) that its sole object is the public good; (3) that it is maintained by public opinion, and not by force. That is to say, public office — all office from the highest to the least — is a public trust — I mean a moral trust, not a syndicate — and it is not private property. It must rest on consent, not on fear, and not on right or privilege. This is not the same thing as an absolute democracy, or an absolute equality. Every citizen has an equal claim to serve the state, but every citizen is not equally able to serve it. And if all did actually serve it at once, the state would be very ill served. The true republic needs the best. By best, it means the worthiest, apart from birth or wealth. And the best must be acknowledged as such by common consent.

It must be allowed that in ancient and modern times this ideal republic has hardly ever been reached, or only for rare and occasional moments. In the Roman republic we know how strong was the hold of privilege, how arrogant were the claims of birth, how desperate the struggles of patrician and plebeian, of the nobles and the proletariat. Indeed, the titles of personal merit to public office were often recognised better in the empire of the Antonines and the Constantines than in the republic of the Catos and the Pompeys.

At Athens, the republic oscillated too often between weak aristocrats and unscrupulous demagogues. And both Athens and Rome were poisoned by the institution of slavery and a vast population of slaves, whom the free minority regarded as their chattels and property. Both states were really narrow aristocracies of free men within unlimited despotisms of serfs.

The mediæval republics, in the same way, rested largely on force; and in no small degree on privilege and birth. The United Provinces of Holland were mainly a plutocracy, until they passed into an hereditary monarchy. In France, the first republic of the

Convention and the Consulate was mainly based on force. Neither in the first nor in the second republic was merit peculiarly honoured. And the third republic has been shaken to its foundations by birth, wealth, and privileged corporations. Europe, alas! never has given the world, does not give it now, the example of a true and typical republic.

We must look to the great republic of the West for a closer approach to the true republican ideal. There indeed we have the principal conditions adequately and permanently recognised. Office — supreme office — is absolutely open to every citizen, whatever his birth, or fortune, or social standing. And this in a degree which has never been accomplished in ancient or modern republics. The whole forces of the republic, again, are devoted to the public benefit of the community as a whole; not to the interests of any order or class of citizens — at least this has been the case since the final extinction of slavery; and, we ought to say, it is at any rate the avowed purpose of the majority. And as to the third condition, you will be ready to say that never did any government rest so entirely on consent; for no government that this world ever yet saw was based upon the free suffrages of twelve millions of independent electors.

I may be asked why did I qualify this statement as to the United States; who can doubt that it is the absolute and perfect type of the true ideal republic? It is not for a foreign visitor to criticise the house of his hosts; but to the philosophers of Europe there are spots even upon the sun of the American commonwealth. If it be true that the offices of the state, from the highest to the lowest, are open to every American citizen, is it clear that they are always filled by the worthiest men that the American continent has reared? If birth and wealth confer no title to power, is it certain that they do not sometimes act as a positive bar to merit? If it be true that the laws and forces of the commonwealth are in principle entirely devoted to the good of all, is it certain that they are not at times captured in the interest of minorities, classes, or corporations? At least, so American authorities of high reputation are believed publicly to maintain. And when we come to the third condition, that the government rests entirely on consent and to no degree on force, it is reported in Europe that this must be qualified somewhat in matters of colour and race. I hope, before I return, I may be convinced that the report is untrue. But in any case, if consent and not force be the rule in the United States, there are now, we hear, some eight or ten millions outside these states, whom the republic governs, but has no intention of admitting to vote.

All these questions are problems in the social economy of states of which thinking men in Europe are anxiously watching the solution. We wait to see how a vast democratic electorate can be educated always to choose its foremost citizens in every service, even though the foremost be the least conspicuous and the least ambitious. We want to see how the state is going to deal with those gigantic corporations, which have taken the place of the feudal barons and royal favourites of modern Europe. And lastly, we wait to see how government of the people, by the people and through the people, will be reconciled with the government of all these millions, whose consent is never going to be asked at all. When we turn in thought to the ideal republic we must have in our mind's eye the highest possible standard. And, with ideal standards before us, no actual republic that men have created can be judged to have reached perfection — no! neither the Athens of Pericles, nor the United States of President McKinley, with all the points of likeness between them that certainly exist.

A republican myself from my youth upwards, I am one who holds that the essence of republic is more bound up with good government than it is with the active share in government by all citizens alike. The interests of all equally are more important than the rights of any section or any individual. Pericles was right when he proudly boasted that their citizens could " recognise the value of personal superiority," for Pericles led the Athenians far more than followed them. Unless the wise man leads and the simple follow his lead, the ideal republic suffers, for its power is not awarded to the most fit. If the blind lead those who see, both the blind and those who see fall into the ditch.

I am, I say, by principle and by conviction, a republican, because the republic is the inevitable and final form of human society — the normal type of intelligent citizenship. It must dominate the future, for the future society must be an industrial society. Whatever else is doubtful, it is certain that the development of industrial life will be the key-note of the generations to come. Now industry is, of its nature, essentially republican; its life is the free coöperation of intelligent masses of men working with good-will to the common interest. Industrial life must ultimately eliminate every remnant of privilege, of caste, of monopoly, of prerogative; for the more highly organised industry becomes, the more perfectly it demands the intelligent and free coöperation of workers. Slavery dies out before the sight of free industry. Military or feudal types of society, with caste, privilege, idleness, mastery blazoned on their mediæval heraldry, may struggle for their ancient rank, but industry will slay them in the end. An industrial world — and the world of the future grows more and more an industrial world — is a republican world. And a republican world is one in which the state belongs to all, exists for all, and lives by the help and good-will of all.

I began to-day with George Washington; and I come back to George Washington at the end. I trust that the American people will evermore look back to Washington as the type of the republican chief. To look back to Washington for guidance and inspiration is to look forward to the future, for it is to fix the eye on the ideal, on the model, which neither you nor any people on this earth have ever yet perfectly attained. During the Presidencies of Washington, this republic was indeed guided by its most capable citizen; not by force, not by submission, but by persuasion and conviction in a way that has hardly ever occurred in the history of mankind, if it were not in the days of Trajan, King Alfred, and William the Silent. If there is any point in his career to be regretted, it is that he did not consent to remain in his great office, so long as his own powers lasted. Personally I believe in republican government; I believe in Presidential rather than parliamentary government; and I believe in retention of office by choice of the citizens so long as capacity to serve them remains.

If Washington's Presidencies give the type of government by the most capable, assuredly they give the type of government by consent of the citizens. Never before or since has authority been wielded by man over his fellow-men with more absolute unanimity of the common desire. He anticipated the great social reformation accomplished in this commonwealth some sixty years after his death, when he freed his own estate by will from the curse of negro slavery. No man that ever bore power over his fellow-citizens shrank with a more scrupulous, more religious horror from the thought of ruling by force instead of by free choice — no man was more truly the republican to the very marrow of his bones, and was less the despot or the master. May the spirit of George Washington, the just, the free, the far-sighted patriot, inspire the people of this commonwealth in all their problems of government; guide them in all the tasks they undertake to wise and prosperous ends; enable them to crown his work when in the words of our English historian, "he founded a democratic republic with no shadow on it of military despotism."

# ABRAHAM LINCOLN

# Abraham Lincoln

ADDRESS AT THE BANQUET, UNION LEAGUE CLUB, CHICAGO, FEBRUARY 22, 1901

MR. PRESIDENT and gentlemen of the Union League Club: I feel myself overwhelmed by the kindness of the reception which I have received and by the hospitality which this great institution has been good enough to afford to me. Although I am now entering upon the close of my life, it is the first time that I have had the opportunity of crossing the Atlantic and seeing with my own eyes the great republic which I have watched with great interest and affection, I may say, for the last fifty years of my life.

I have many American friends; I have received many invitations to visit them in this country; I have never been able to accept those invitations, but when, last autumn, I had the great honour of being invited by the president of the Union League Club to speak on this memorable day, the birthday of Washington, and that invitation was conveyed to me by the highly popular and respected representative of the American nation in England, Mr. Choate, I felt, sir, that that invitation was that which our politicians speak of, when they are called by the sovereign of our country at

Windsor Castle, as a royal command. I felt, sir, as if I had received a command to speak, with however humble a voice, to the American people, to represent the sympathy and regard that our nation feels for the American republic and its infinite destinies in the future, and above all, to tell them of the admiration, of the profound homage with which the founder of the American republic is looked upon by all rational people of Great Britain to-day.

I well knew that it was from no thought of merit of my own that I had been honoured by this invitation, but, having received it and having had the advantage of listening to the words of our great orators, Mr. Cobden and Mr. Bright, whom I well remember, whom I have often heard speak with so bold a spirit during the great struggle that was endured by this nation in my own youth — I felt that I was bound to come forward to-day and say all that in my heart I have felt of their people and of their great founder. This city of Chicago appeals to me in a very especial manner above all the other cities of the United States, for the personal reason that I believe that I am myself, at this moment, older than the city of Chicago; because I am told in the histories that at my birth it was a village of but one hundred inhabitants, and when I was a young man, taking my degree in college, it was a very small town, hardly known on the other side of the Atlantic. But I come now and I see that it is undoubtedly the second city in the Union. Its history is one of the most remarkable facts in the material development of the nineteenth century; its wealth, its power, its population portend almost an infinite development in the future. I have now been able to see with my own eyes and through the instrumentality of the many friends here about me, the culture, intellectual development, and patriotic spirit which this city has already developed.

I was deeply interested this morning in seeing that remarkable gathering when the young people of this great city were brought together to have instilled into their minds ideas of true patriotic spirit and the sense of devotion to their duties in order to become worthy citizens of this republic. Now I should be very sorry if it were thought that what I have been saying of Washington to-day was in any sense addressed for the moment or to meet the audience to which I had the honour of speaking. On the contrary, I well know that the spirit of Washington, his courage, his patriotic interest to the people of his country, have been carried on in later years by his successors in that great office, and I may recall, perhaps, my own interest as a young man many years ago during the great struggle in which this nation was concerned, the thrill of sympathy, the sense of shock which we received when we heard of the death of that great successor of Washington, whose portrait, I see, adorns the rooms of this club. I was present upon the occasion of the announcement of the death of that great President of the republic. We called a meeting in the largest available hall in London, which was draped in black for the occasion, and our foremost politicians came forward and spoke of the admiration with which they had regarded his career, and of the profound sympathy that they felt for the tremendous struggle with which this nation was engaged. I may say Abraham Lincoln was always to me, in my youth, the type of the republican chief, and I looked upon him as indeed a worthy successor of the founder of the republic himself.

I should like to recall a few remarks that I made in a little volume which, I dare say, very few people ever read, and of which I don't suppose there is a single copy in existence, except the one in my possession. If I venture to inflict upon you a few comments of mine, it is only for this purpose, to convince you that during that great struggle, which is now very nearly forty years ago, there were many of us who followed every incident of that immense crisis with all the feelings that animated you whom I see before me, or perhaps, as most of you have evidently the advantage of me in years, which animated your fathers and the previous generation. I don't know how many of you actually took part in that heroic struggle, but to us it came home precisely as if we were engaged in it from day to day ourselves. And the end of the President in that great crisis was to us as deeply affecting as it was to any one of you or to your fathers.

It is now nearly forty years ago since I published in England the following remarks: —

". . . The great struggle which has for ever decided the cause of slavery of man to man, is, beyond all question, the most critical which the world has seen since the great revolutionary outburst. If ever there was a question which was to test political capacity and honesty it was this. A true statesman, here if ever, was bound to forecast truly the issue, and to judge faithfully the cause at stake. We know now, it is beyond dispute, that the cause which won was certain to win in the end, that its reserve force was absolutely without limit, that its triumph was one of the turning-points in modern civilisation. It was morally certain to succeed, and it did succeed with an overwhelming and mighty success. From first to last both might and right went all one way. The people of England went wholly that way. The official classes went wholly some other way.

"One of the great key-notes of England's future is simply this — what will be her relations with that great republic? If the two branches of the Anglo-Saxon race are to form two phases of one political movement, their welfare and that of the world will be signally promoted. If their courses are marred by jealousies or contests, both will be fatally retarded. Real confidence and sympathy extended to that people in the hour of their trial would have forged an eternal bond between us. To discredit and distrust them, then, was to sow deep the seeds of antipathy. Yet, although a union in feeling was of importance so great, although so little would have secured it, the governing classes of England wantonly did all they could to foment a breach.

"A great political judgment fell upon a race of men, our own brothers; the inveterate social malady they inherited came to a crisis. We watched it gather with exultation and insult. There fell on them the most terrible necessity which can befall men, the necessity of sacrificing the flower of their citizens in civil war, of tearing up their civil and social system by the roots, of transforming the most peaceful type of society into the most military. We magnified and shouted over every disaster; we covered them with insult; we filled the world with ominous forebodings and unjust accusations. There came on them one awful hour when the powers of evil seemed almost too strong; when any but a most heroic race would have sunk under the blows of their traitorous kindred. We chose that moment to give actual succour to their enemy, and stabbed them in the back with a wound which stung their pride even more than it crippled their strength. They displayed the most splendid examples of energy and fortitude which the modern world has seen, with which the defence of Greece against Asia, and of France against Europe, alone can be compared in the whole annals of mankind. They developed almost ideal civic virtues and gifts; generosity, faith, firmness; sympathy the most affecting, resources the most exhaustless, ingenuity the most magical. They brought forth the most beautiful and heroic character who in recent times has ever led a nation, the only blameless type of the statesman since the days of Washington. Under him they created the purest model of government which has yet been seen on the earth — a whole nation throbbing into one great heart and brain, one great heart and brain giving unity and life to a whole nation. The hour of their success came; unchequered in the completeness of its triumph, unsullied by any act of vengeance, hallowed by a great martyrdom."

Mr. President, I have only ventured to refer to those words of mine in order that I may assure you and the members of this Club that I have been deeply interested in the fortunes of the great American republic ever since I was a youth fresh from school and college. I have felt throughout the whole of my life the same sympathy with the destinies of this great nation, and I shall carry back to my own people the assurance of the friendliness and kindness with which they always receive an English guest, and also the sense that in all things intellectual, moral, and spiritual the two peoples are indissolubly united in thought and in idea, whilst in things practical and in the political sphere they hope to preserve for ever a thoroughly good understanding and a common fellowship, working their own national conceptions out in independent lines.

THE MILLENARY OF KING ALFRED
d. 901

# The Millenary of King Alfred (d. 901)

ADDRESS AT JOHNS HOPKINS UNIVERSITY, BALTIMORE

WITHIN a few months, in the present year, the various peoples in both hemispheres and on either side of the Equator who speak our English tongue, will unite in commemorating the thousandth anniversary of the death of King Alfred — the purest, noblest, most venerable hero of which their race can boast. There are few other names in the records of human civilisation, the memory of which has been so permanent, so unbroken, so definite, and at the same time so certain. And there is certainly no other character in history whose image remains to this day perfectly heroic, faultless, majestic, and saintly in all relations of public or of private life.

History, especially the remorseless criticism of modern scholarship, has torn the halo from many a famous hero, and has exposed the fraud or superstition which built up so many of our cherished legends and anecdotes. But if it has cleared the memory of Alfred from some pleasing and some trivial myths, which were solemnly believed by our fathers, it has really made the historic Alfred a more heroic and impressive figure than the legendary figure of our boyhood. The true Alfred is even greater than the poetic Alfred.

And whatever records have "leaped to light," as our poet has it, and whatever tales have been flung aside in the process of research, no weakness, no crime, no error, no falsehood, no cruelty have ever been revealed in his career.

It is true that the *scale* of the achievements of such mighty men of old as Alexander, Julius Cæsar, and Charlemagne, is immeasurably greater, and their permanent influence on human history as a whole has been infinitely wider, as their tradition is older and more diffused amongst the nations to-day. But their influence is to be traced in so many undefined and indirect results that it can with difficulty be grasped in a manner quite definite, with the same intensity, national and racial, as that of Alfred. And undoubtedly no one of these immortal founders of kingdoms and of eras, nor can any other historic founder of a nation, compare with our Alfred in beauty of soul and in variety of genius and grace.

We are quite justified also in speaking of the history of Alfred as conspicuously certain and clear. An immense amount of controversy has been carried on in England, America, and Germany as to certain details of Alfred's life — the exact dates of his death and even of his birth are disputed, the extent of his learning, the age at which he learned to read and to understand Latin, a variety of characteristic anecdotes, and some personal peculiarities and feats. It is true that doubts continue as to the authenticity and genuineness of our principal authority, the *Life by*

*Asser*, which, at best, is mixed with interpolations, misconceptions, and errors. And doubts exist as to Alfred's being in any sense the author of some books attributed to him, and as to what degree he is the author of books in which he certainly had a hand.

But all these things are more or less superficial and practically unimportant. The date of Alfred's death might be of great significance if certain events occurred at this time, or if certain men or movements ought or ought not to be treated as contemporary with him. But inasmuch as we know almost nothing of any real mark as taking place in any of the years 899, 900, or 901, it becomes a mere arithmetical or paleographical problem to which of the three we attribute the death. Absolutely nothing can turn on it, any more than whether he died on the 24th or the 26th of October. Historians have long agreed that 901 was the date of Alfred's death, — how, where, and why he died at fifty-two they knew not. The whole controversy turns on such questions as whether the scribe in a manuscript of the *Saxon Chronicle* put the date 901 exactly in the right line of his margin, and at what day of what month the West Saxons at that time ordinarily counted the commencement of the year. After studying a great deal of warm controversy on the subject, I incline to the view that the year 900 is the more likely to be correct. But the matter is to me too much like the solution of a chess problem; and I rather regret to see so much ingenuity exhausted on the point. It would be far more to the purpose if they could tell us whether Alfred was six feet high, or if his eyes were blue or dark. None of these things have we any means of knowing; and it is a pity to draw off the attention of the public from the grand and certain facts of Alfred's career. Since the Christian world continues to commemorate the birth of Christ at a date which has long been known to be historically inaccurate, the Commemoration Committee wisely resolved to adhere to the recognised and popular date.

I confess that I feel little interest in solving these petty problems of detail — all the more that I very much doubt if they ever can be finally settled. For myself, after no little reading and hesitation, I incline to believe that the *Life of Asser* is substantially genuine, and is accurate in the main; though it is certainly corrupt, defaced by palpable forgeries, and some original errors. I incline to believe that the pretty story of the boy Alfred learning to read has foundation in fact, though the circumstances and his own age at the time present hopeless inconsistencies and confusion. It is quite possible that the legend about the cakes may have had some basis of truth, but we can say no more. It may have come from a popular ballad, as probably came the story of the harper in the Danes' camp. The story of S. Neot, and the school at Oxford, are known to be pure inventions of later ages. The name of the King has certainly been given to some books which he did not write. And some of his deeds are demonstrably impossible; and others which are possible, seem to have been unknown to his own age.

But, when all deductions are made and all doubtful tales are rejected, enough remains to give us a complete picture of the man himself and unimpeachable evidence of his essential achievements. There is the record of the *Chronicle* during Alfred's life, as trustworthy as the commentaries of Cæsar and probably dictated by the King himself. There is the general picture of character to be extracted from Asser, his friend and companion. We have undoubted writings by Alfred himself — the *Pastoral Care* with its preface, the *Orosius* with its insertions, and above all the *Boethius* with its abundant original matter — so largely an autobiography or the personal meditations of the King himself. Lastly, we have the immense body of Saxon and English annals and poems testifying to a persistent tradition, if not to positive facts. Out of all these sources we get a perfectly definite and thoroughly consistent picture of a nature of singular beauty and power; of a career as warrior, statesman, churchman, and lawgiver of incalculable importance to the existence and formation of the nation he inspired and ruled. The principal deeds of Alfred as king are quite as certain as those of Charlemagne, or William the Conqueror, or Edward I. And we know the inner spirit of Alfred far better than we shall ever know theirs.

This is the age of minute historical research and we ought to be on our guard never to become its dupes or its slaves. Of course absolute truth and the most scrupulous accuracy of fact are quite indispensable; and deliberate neglect of either must be the final condemnation of anyone found guilty thereof. Every historian must desire to have over his labours the epitaph that the late Bishop Creighton is said to have composed for himself — " he tried to write true history." But the extraordinary zeal with which paleography is pursued and the infinite sub-divisions of this curious learning have caused historical problems to be treated too much in sectional and mechanical modes, which make us too prone to trust our general judgment to mere technical *experts*. We have seen the dangers of giving too much weight in a criminal trial to the *expert* graphologist, or professor of " cheiromancy," who is positive that a line of handwriting is the work of one particular person, or the expert in painting who knows how much of a picture is genuine and how much is spurious. A famous judge was wont to say that witnesses in a patent case might be divided into three classes — (1) liars, (2) d—d liars, and (3) " experts " — to which someone added a fourth class consisting of one too famous professional witness.

What I mean is, that due attention should be paid to the opinion of qualified experts in handwriting, paleography, style, dialect, and so forth, especially when they agree, which they rarely do. But many other considerations have to be taken into account, on which few " experts " are at all expert. One scholar says — Homer never speaks of writing. *Ergo*, the

*Iliad* and the *Odyssey* were preserved solely by oral tradition. Then comes a learned archæologist who finds some marks which he cannot decipher, and which he believes to be much earlier than Homer. *Ergo*, he says, Homer's poems were written by the poet. The bone of a Cave-bear is found with some rude figures on it: this proves man, they say, to have been an artist twenty thousand years ago. A copy of the Saxon *Chronicle* is said to have the date in its margin the eighth of an inch too high. *Ergo*, Alfred died in 899 and not in 901. I express no opinion on anything of these discoveries. I am far from undervaluing them, and feel that they merit close attention. But I say — Not too fast; there are many other things to consider; there are hardly ten men accessible whose opinion on these points is conclusive; and there are a dozen modes in which the fact now observed may be explained without our accepting the momentous conclusions that are claimed. A mere expert, like fire, is a good servant, but a bad master.

I deal with these points because some persons have suggested as objection to the Millenary Commemoration this year, that it is more probable that Alfred died in 899, or in 900, and not in 901. Again it has been suggested that Alfred was born not in 849, as all the ordinary histories tell us, but in 842, which would make him seven years older. This would make things easier all round. It would be far more reasonable if Ethelwulf sent his son, then aged thirteen, to Rome, instead of sending a child of four on so long and difficult a journey. And he might very well have won the beautiful book and learned to read at the age of twelve with his own mother Osburga, who might then have been living. In that case Alfred would have been thirty when he began to reign, instead of twenty-two, and would have been fifty-eight, or even fifty-nine, at his death, which makes more conceivable the enormous amount of his life's work. But against this stands the distinct statement of the *Chronicle* and also of Asser in his *Life*, the authority for both of which must have been Alfred himself, that he began to reign at the age of twenty-two.

Now, I refer to these points, still in dispute by the experts, simply to show that the matters which are doubtful about Alfred are not matters which affect our estimate of Alfred's character or Alfred's achievements. There are people who will object to anything and give all kinds of trivial reasons. A very great personage, who is a statesman as well as an historian, says that Alfred "is a myth." He might as well say St. Paul "is a myth," because he does not believe in the tradition of his foot marks in the Mamertine Prison in Rome or of the — *Domine, Quo Vadis?* — in the *fuori le Mura* anecdote. There are many things as to St. Paul, of which we are not certain, and some stories which we know to be fictions. And so, there are some things about Alfred of which we are not certain, and some things which we know to be fiction. But St. Paul and Alfred both wrote some authentic and genuine pieces in which their whole souls are shown. Both had intimate companions who certainly recorded the essential facts of their lives. And, though we are not quite certain in which of three years Alfred died, nor of what he died, nor where, or what was his exact age at death, we do know for certain how vast was the work of his life in the history of his country, and we do know what the real Alfred was as hero, statesman, and saint.

Again, there are people who grumble about any millenary, and others who sneer at the word itself. Well! *millenary* is quite as natural and correct a term as *centenary* — and of centenaries we hear more than enough. In the nature of things, there will be very few millenaries possible. The mere fact that the memory of a great thinker or statesman keeps bright for a thousand years is a striking phenomenon which we ought to emphasise with all our power. It is the death always, not the birth, we should commemorate. What had happened in the world when Alfred saw the light? It was a time of confusion, trouble, and despair. What happened when Alfred died, was this. The purest spirit that ever spoke our mother tongue lay in its last rest. England was saved from barbarism and from heathendom. The civilisation of England began in earnest — and for a thousand years it has grown larger and grander.

Let us turn to the things of which we are certain and wherein Alfred's greatness is clear as the sun at noon. He was a mighty soldier — a hero — with consummate genius for war. An historian who has written an excellent *History of the Art of War* for the Middle Ages, has treated Alfred as warrior, and made clear all the essential points, though many details of his tactics still remain obscure. Alfred's youth was passed in the midst of the death-struggle of Saxons and Angles with the Danes and Vikings. For two generations they had been cutting England to pieces, and whilst he was a boy, they had begun to fix themselves in fortified camps along the coast. The Saxons had no forts, no fleet, no regular armies, and but few soldiers wearing defensive armour and trained to war. The Vikings had all these. They were pirates, adventurers, conquerors, with a genius for enterprise and desultory fighting, splendid seamen, trained warriors of undaunted courage and resource. And they had now learned the use of horses, more as mounted infantry than regular cavalry. In fact they were much like the Boers under de Wet; and the Saxons were like the British at Majuba or Stormberg.

England and the Continent, what we now call France, Belgium, and Holland, were equally at the mercy of these terrible invaders. And the period from Alfred's birth to his thirtieth year was the darkest time of all for Christian Europe. The heirs of Charles the Great, the heirs of our Egbert, were alike defeated in turn — London, Winchester, Paris, and Tours were sacked and destroyed. Then York was stormed, the Northumbrian kings slain and their kingdom blotted out. Then the Mercian kingdom was attacked, and the East Anglian king slaughtered. Alfred was twenty-two when the " grand army " of the Vikings descended upon Wessex, seized Reading, and entrenched themselves along the Thames. They were carrying all before them, when Alfred and his brother Ethelred, then king of Wessex, came up with them at Ashdown, in the " Vale of the White Horse." We have prime accounts of the battle: how Alfred would not wait for the king who remained to hear mass, but charged up hill " as furious as a wild boar " — how the battle raged till nightfall — how the heathen were smitten hip and thigh — how their king, five earls, and thousands of pagans were slain, and the enemy routed and chased for two days. This grand victory is always ascribed to Alfred's personal valour and leadership. He was but twenty-two.

But this glorious victory did not save Wessex. In a few weeks the Danes rallied, defeated Ethelred again and again, and finally killed him, when Alfred became King at twenty-two. He was now in the thick of war, driven back from Berkshire into Wiltshire, with incessant battles, not unfrequent victories in the field, followed by disastrous retreats, as his worn forces grew smaller and more exhausted. In that year, says the veracious *Chronicle*, dictated perhaps by Alfred himself, nine general battles were fought against the army south of Thames, besides frequent raids, and nine earls and one king of the Vikings were slain.

But, after this mutual slaughter, both sides were exhausted; and Alfred obtained a truce for Wessex perhaps by a judicious subsidy. It was nothing but a truce, as he well knew, but it gave him invaluable time to recruit. His eye of genius perceived that he must stop this endless flow from the north, and deprive the invaders of their command of the sea, which had given them the advantage of mobility. Alfred built galleys and long ships, and brought in Danes and Norsemen from across the Channel to teach his people seamanship. He now began to win naval victories, and protect his own southern coasts, on which one hundred and twenty galleys of the Vikings were wrecked after an engagement with Alfred's formidable fleet. But whilst the King was in the far west, where he overcame the Danes at Exeter, a new body from the northeast burst into Wessex and planted themselves in Wiltshire. The Saxons were panic-stricken, and many fled over seas, whilst Alfred, with his body-guard, took refuge in the marshes of the Parret and entrenched himself, as in early days the Danes used to do, at Athelney in Somersetshire. Issuing from his stronghold, the King massed the levies of Somerset, Wilts, and Hampshire, and in the decisive battle of Eddington he overthrew the Danes with great slaughter, and drove them to their base at Chippenham. Here they were besieged and surrendered at discretion. Guthrum and thirty of his chiefs consented to be baptized. He took the name of Athelstan: they swore fealty to Alfred, and consented to withdraw to East Anglia and settle down in Norfolk and Suffolk. This Treaty of Wedmore in 878 was the foundation of Alfred's new settlement of England. It was a momentous date: the civilisation, compound races, unity, and peace of our island all take their origin from this settlement, which was as statesmanlike in conception as it was magnanimous in spirit.

Alfred was now twenty-nine, and he had been King just seven years. He was already the darling of his people and the founder of our nation. He had now learned all the tactics of the Vikings, and he could beat them at their own manœuvres. He now possessed sea power, and could meet them before they reached our shores; and he used the years of peace to organise a navy far superior to theirs. Resisting the strong temptation to exterminate the heathen invaders whom he had beaten in a dozen fights, he induced them to make peace on advantageous terms, to become Christian, to settle down on the land and take to fixed and civilised life instead of piracy and war, and he consented to their retaining the east and east centre of the kingdom north of Thames, out of which, indeed, they had driven Mercians and Anglians. Guthrum's East Anglia became a Christian "buffer-state" between the Vikings and Wessex; and it has proved the nucleus of one of the stoutest and most important races in the complex history of Great Britain.

Alfred now set to work with all the energy of his soul, and the insight of consummate genius to take care that the new and settled Danish race should not be disturbed or perverted by fresh heathen invaders. He laboured to develop his fleet, taking command of his ships in person, and he devised a new type of cruiser, — "long ships nigh twice as long as those of the Danes, with sixty oars or more, steadier and swifter, as well as higher out of the water, on a design of his own, quite unlike that of Frisians or Danes." In one summer with his new warships he destroyed more than twenty Viking ships along the southern coast.

But he saw the need for fortresses on land as well as for a navy at sea. He built a system of strong places, fencing in the towns and raising stockades at spots in the country. He rebuilt London by restoring the old Roman walls and filling it with a new colony of warlike settlers. It thus formed a post north of Thames which commanded the approach to Essex and East Anglia, as Calais in the fifteenth century commanded the entrance into France. Alfred had many wars in the last twenty years of his reign, but their whole character and strategy is altered. The invaders are continually stopped and dispersed at sea; they never capture any important town; they are never able to post themselves firmly and occupy a district. They are in the true sense (not in the British official sense) "marauders"; and they are driven backwards and forwards from Thames to the Exe, from Chester to Essex before the eagle swoop of the unwearied and invincible King. Alfred's most brilliant campaign, fought all across England, is difficult indeed to explain, by reason of its rapid changes and great area. It was that which ended in 896, in the forty-seventh year of his life and the twenty-fifth of his reign.

Along with his system of fortifications, Alfred reorganised the militia of the kingdom, dividing it into a stationary or garrison part, and a mobilised and campaigning part. It was a rude anticipation of the feudal system of defensive war. At his accession the gallant Saxons had been a mere crowd of half-armed countrymen. In ten or fifteen years of war and of military organisation, Alfred had created the nucleus of a regular army, with adequate fortified bases, and something like a knighthood or chivalry, a rudimentary feudal militia. With this, in the later part of his reign, his campaigns are a series of decisive blows, his battles are crushing defeats of the enemy, and his command of the field is triumphant at every point. One of his most brilliant feats was capturing without ships a Danish fleet which had pushed up the river Lea. He barred the river, defended its banks with stockades, and forced the Vikings to escape by land, leaving behind them their ships. Since the capture of British ships by French cavalry on the ice in the great war, there has seldom been so singular an exploit. In fact during the later life of the King the Norsemen hardly ventured to trouble our island. They turned aside to Flanders, Normandy, and the coasts of the Continent.

" For the last four years of his life," says Professor Oman, " Alfred was undisturbed save by trifling raids of small squadrons, which he brushed off with ease by means of the new fleet of ' great ships ' which he had built. The work of defence was done : Wessex was saved, and with Wessex the

English nationality. In a few years the King's gallant son, Edward the Elder, was to take the offensive against the old enemy, and to repay on the Danelagh all the evils that England had suffered during the miserable years of the ninth century. That such triumphs lay within his power was absolutely and entirely the work of his great father, who had turned defeat into victory, brought order out of chaos, and left the torn and riven kingdom that he had inherited transformed into the best organised and most powerful state in Western Europe."

Is Alfred "a myth" now, I ask. It is true that some of the details of these campaigns are doubtful; not a few are obscure to explain. But the whole of the points which I have briefly summarised are certain and clear. They may dispute which Merton is meant, what Eddington now is, and why Alfred was beaten so soon after the battle of Ashdown. But all these things are unimportant. The essential facts are plain; they are certain. And they are enough to raise Alfred as warrior to the same level as Henry V, or Cromwell, or Marlborough, — aye, almost as seaman to the level of Blake and Nelson, for he grasped the idea of sea power and realised its decisive effects. And they raise him as statesman and founder of nations to the level of the Conqueror, and Edward I, or the Protector. They recast our nation. Alfred was its original creator.

Turn to his achievements as king. When he came to the throne at twenty-two, having seen the death of his father and his three brothers within thirteen years, it was the darkest hour of the West Saxons. Northumbria, Mercia, East Anglia, and parts of Wessex had been desolated; the abbeys sacked; schools, churches, homesteads in ruins. Northern, Central, and Eastern England was in possession of the Danes, and Wessex lay at their mercy; "the people submitted to them, save King Alfred, — he with a little band withdrew into the woods and swamps." It was the gravest crisis to which England ever was exposed, for conquest by the ferocious pagans would have meant the postponement of British civilisation for ages. Once established in our island, the Danes would have been the scourge of Northern Europe. From this supreme disaster Alfred — and he alone — saved England, preserved Europe.

No sooner had he settled Guthrum and his host at East Anglia, which secured the incorporation of a Norseman race with the Saxon and with England, than Alfred set to work to restore his desolated land. His treasury was empty, his towns were in ruins, civil government was paralysed. He built churches, abbeys, schools; he repeopled waste districts. He reorganised justice, making the judges the ministers of the sovereign, and subject to his final appeal. As legislator he recast and fused the Saxon, Anglian, and Kentish laws or "dooms," so that unity of civil law stimulated the fusion of central, eastern, and southern Anglo-Saxons. His system of laws, of which we have authentic records, which a learned German, Dr. Liebermann, has now edited with scholarly precision, is a model of wise, cautious, and broad legal reform. He is full of anxiety not to make abrupt innovation, to impose nothing strange or unwelcome, and to enact no command which could not be maintained by public opinion.

The restoration of London was a stroke of profound statecraft. By it he blocked the raids of the Norsemen up the Thames, by which they had been wont to penetrate into Surrey, Middlesex, and Berkshire. By it he obtained an impregnable fortress, north of Thames, by which he could control East Anglia. How little could he foresee what London was to become a thousand years after his time. Perhaps he might have doubted if he was wise, could he now return to earth to see all that this huge agglomeration of buildings has become. But the restoration of the ancient city, which the Roman historian describes as "especially famous for the crowd of its merchants and their wares" — the city which in Alfred's day counted nearly a thousand years of continuous life, but which had lain desolate for thirty-five years since its destruction by the Norsemen about the time of Alfred's birth — the city which now counts nearly two thousand years of existence, and is now the vastest accumulation of men that has ever been recorded in authentic history — the restoration of London, I say, destined to be the barrier of the Danes and the gateway into Mercia, and finally the emporium of the world, was the master-stroke of a great far-seeing genius.

He showed himself in the rest of his policy the

same far-sighted and organising creator of a new nation. The Christianised Danes of East Anglia soon learned to look with admiration and awe on his power. Alfred in the second half of his reign ruled over a compact state reaching from the Channel up into Southwestern England as far as Lancashire, with fortresses along the Thames, along the rivers of the west, and up to Chester on the north. English Mercia which he created and which was so admirably ruled by his able daughter Ethelfleda and her husband, Ethelred, formed a new buffer-state between the Danes of the Danelagh in East Anglia and the Britons of Cornwall and Wales. Alfred made no attempt formally to annex either Cornwall, or Wales, or East Anglia, or Northumbria. But his paramount influence over all was felt, and they recognised the supreme influence of the organic, civilised, progressive kingdom of Wessex. Alfred created for his descendants a united England not by conquest, not by fraud — but by wisdom, justice, and moral greatness.

But the genius and serene humanity of Alfred was not content with our little island. He was European, Catholic, imperial, in the highest and purest meaning of these words. In truth, he recognised that the petty island of which he was the predominant chief needed to be sustained and vivified by the larger and more ancient culture of Southern Europe and even of the East. He who had been a boy at Rome, hallowed by the hand of the great Pope Leo IV, he who had crossed Europe twice, and had been at the Court of the Frank king, the great grand-daughter of Charlemagne becoming his step-mother, used every means to connect our island with the culture of the Continent. He brought over learned men from France and Germany; he sent constant missions and tribute to Rome; he sent bold navigators to the North Cape and the Baltic; he was in communication with the Patriarch of Jerusalem, and the better opinion is that he sent a mission to the Christian churches in India. East and West were filled with a profound impression of the lofty and religious enthusiasm of the West-Saxon king — the new Charlemagne of Britain who dreamed of an intellectual commerce between the ancient world and the new world, between the East and the West. This was to be a true imperialist — to found a world-wide empire of sympathy, knowledge, and ideas — not one of bloodshed, domination, and ruin.

Alfred's energy and culture seem to have been of that general and encyclopædic kind which marks only the greatest and rarest of mankind. War, hunting, poetry, music, literature, architecture, mechanics, geography, law, prayer, and ceremonial seem alike to have employed his interests. He built churches, courts, schools, monasteries for men and for women; he designed ships, lamps to read by, and machines to record the time. Only the other day at Oxford I had in my hand the very copy of the *Pastoral Care* which he sent to Worcester Cathedral, for he tells us he had one sent to each diocese in his kingdom; and I handled that curious and perfect remnant of his personal effects — the Jewel, which, with enamel work and delicate gold filigree, bears the inscription — *Alfred had me worked*. The precise form of his buildings we know not. It is doubtful if a single stone of his actual construction remains, at least not any that is visible to-day. But the traditions, anecdotes, and things ascribed to the King, even if we can trust few particulars of them, exactly testify to the general belief in his extraordinary range of interest. Alfred lived in an age of very few books, of most meagre learning and of rudimentary simplicity of life — an age when a man of consummate genius and of inexhaustible energy could master almost everything of value that was to be known, and almost everything essential that had to be made or done. I doubt if recorded history tells of any men who in range of interest and variety of power were quite the equals of Alfred, unless it be Alexander, Julius Cæsar, and Charles the Great, and perhaps Bonaparte. And if Julius, Alexander, and Bonaparte greatly surpassed Alfred in scientific acquirements, they were immeasurably inferior to him in grace of nature and beauty of soul. And if the mighty Charles towered above Alfred in force and in breadth of space, he could not compare with the West-Saxon saint in exquisite purity or in spiritual elevation. Alfred, it is truly said, was the only perfect man of action in the annals of mankind.

It is in his own writings that we know the true Alfred best. Julius and Bonaparte have left us memoirs of themselves more ample than Alfred's; but neither of them open to us their own souls with such candour and truth. The authentic writings of our King are ample to shew us how he looked on the world, on his duty, on his aspirations, and on his Creator. No man has left us his thoughts with such entire openness of heart, if it be not St. Paul, St. Augustine, St. Bernard, Marcus Aurelius, or King David. The so-called *Boethius* of Alfred, one third of which are his own original meditations, is as beautiful in expression as it is noble in thought. It is certain that these are the genuine words of the royal saint. And neither ancient moralist nor scriptural homily has ever exceeded them in dignity and elevation. Listen to these words: —

"Power is never a good thing save its possessor be good; for when power is beneficent, this is due to the man who wields it. Therefore it is that a man never by his authority attains to virtue and excellence, but by reason of his virtue and excellence he attains to authority and power. No man is better for his power, but for his skill he is good, if he is good, and for his skill he is worthy of power, if he is worthy of it. Study Wisdom then, and when ye have learned it, contemn it not, for I tell you that by its means ye may without fail attain to power, yea, even though not desiring it. Ye need not take thought for power nor endeavour after it; for if ye are only wise and good, it will follow you, even though ye seek it not. Tell me now, O Mind, what is the height of thy desire in wealth and power? Is it not this present life and the perishable wealth that we before spoke of? O ye foolish men, do ye know what riches are, and power, and worldly weal? They are your lords and rulers, not ye theirs."

This is how the King understands his own royal office. He says : —

"O Philosophy, thou knowest that I never greatly delighted in the possession of earthly power, nor longed for this authority, but I desired instruments and materials to carry out the work I was set to do, which was that I should virtuously and fittingly administer the authority committed to me. Now, no man, as thou knowest, can get full play for his natural gifts, nor conduct and administer government, unless he hath fit tools, and the raw material to work upon. By material I mean that which is necessary to the exercise of natural powers; thus a king's raw material and instruments of rule are a well-peopled land, and he must have men of prayer, men of war, and men of work. As thou knowest, without these tools no king may display his special talent. . . . I have desired material for the exercise of government that my talents and my power might not be forgotten, for every good gift and every power soon groweth old and is no more heard of, if Wisdom be not in them. Without Wisdom no faculty can be fully brought out, for whatsoever is done unwisely can never be accounted as skill. To sum up all, I may say that it has ever been my desire to live honourably while I was alive, and after my death to leave to them that should come after me my memory in good works."

That memory in good works of the Saxon hero has now lasted a thousand years after his death; and is more definite, more inspiring, more sacred to us to-day than it has ever been in the ten centuries through which it has survived. Shall we, the hundred millions on both sides of the Atlantic who speak the tongue that Alfred spoke, who are of the same blood and kindred, suffer to fade away the memory of one who was the noblest type of our race and traditions. In this age of Progress and of never-ending pursuit of new things, new men, new ideas, we feel ever more and more in the bottom of our minds, the need to base these on just traditions of the Past. Ours is the age of Progress; but it is also the age of History, and of due commemoration of all that in the Past has been surest, purest, and best. Ours is an age of Hero-worship in the true and wise sense of the term, the reverent honour of our real teachers, founders, and chiefs. To a nation the quality of its Ideals are everything — the Ideals are more vital to a people than they are to a man; for he has personal and individual models before him from his youth. By Ideals I mean that which a people admires and seeks to imitate, to reproduce, to follow.

The intellectual, spiritual, scientific heroes of our nation and race receive, as it is, abundant honour and consideration. The Shakespeares and Miltons, the Newtons and the Darwins, the Gregorys and the Bernards are amply remembered. But the kings, warriors, and statesmen too often bring divisions of nation, creed, and school of opinion. The Richelieus and the Cromwells, the Fredericks and the Bonapartes, even the Turgots and the Washingtons have left some memories of strife and defeat behind them. There is hardly in all modern history a name which does not rouse some embers of passion in one or other quarter of those who suffered at the hand of the soldier or the ruler. The name of Alfred can awaken no memory but one of gratitude and affection. It is bound up with no struggle of Protestant against Catholic, or of Celt against Saxon, of people against king, of reformer against reactionist, of rich against poor, of weak against the strong. His memory is one record of unsullied beneficence, of piety without superstition, of valour without cruelty, of government without oppression.

Without hyperbole, without boasting, we may say that it is the most ancient, the most continuous, the most definite memory in all Christian history. If that of the Catholic church and of its founders and chiefs is more ancient and also more extended, it is the memory of an institution and its influence and effects are less locally defined. If the memory of Charlemagne is grander and more diffused, the sequence of his authority is more broken and dispersed. But the unbroken effect of Alfred's life and work can be traced with precision over a thousand years, and for another thousand years, we may predict, it will continue to flourish and enlarge.

How vast is this antiquity of tradition compared with anything in modern history. It is but two years ago that the great Republic of the West celebrated the first centenary of their immortal founder's death — George Washington. The French Republic celebrated its first centenary just twelve years ago. The kingdom of Italy is forty years old. The German Empire is thirty years old; and it has just been celebrating the second centenary of the kingdom of Prussia in 1701. The second centenary! Why! Alfred, at his birth, had a royal descent from kings of the West-Saxons of nearly four centuries; and we now count ten centuries more since his death. The blood of Alfred has descended from generation to generation in thirty-three degrees down to King Edward the Seventh, who can trace his ancestry and his throne in a long succession of nearly fourteen centuries up to the first Saxon conquerors of our island. I set as little store as Alfred himself by mere antiquity of birth — (high birth is of the mind, he says, not of the flesh) — nor do I rate extravagantly mere effluxion of time. But the historic imagination confers a halo on exalted virtue and genius when it finds it charged with tremendous responsibilities and tasks, when it is mellowed by the veil of a venerable antiquity of age.

The thousandth year of such a memory ought not to pass without a commemoration worthy of such a name. Of the walls which he raised, the halls wherein he dwelt, the churches and the towers that he built, it is difficult to-day to trace more than a few stones. His tomb even was twice removed, and at last was laid in a new abbey some distance from the spot where his people laid it. We have sought sorrowing the place where our hero was laid. In the last century the very spot where his coffin was placed could have been identified. But rather more than a hundred years ago the very foundations of Hyde Abbey were removed. And to-day no man can tell us where the dust of the noblest of Englishmen was scattered. I have searched the spot in vain, though I believe that the very acre of ground in which that sacred dust still rests can still with certainty be traced. But Winchester, the home and capital of the hero-king of Wessex, will not forget him. And in a few months the grandest colossal statue in our country will be set up hard by the foundation of his castle and his church; and it will bear witness for ages to come that Englishmen have not yet forgotten the founder of their national greatness and the noblest soul that England ever bore.

# THE WRITINGS OF KING ALFRED
d. 901

# The Writings of King Alfred

(Died 901)

Address given at Harvard College, Mass., March, 1901

In the great days of antique culture, when the citizen of Athens, coming from the Academus or the Stoa, found himself in the Museum of Alexandria, or in the schools of Syracuse, Magna Græcia, Asia Minor, or Tyre, he felt that he was still in his own country, both intellectually and morally, whatever might be the state or nation to which he had travelled. He and his guests spoke but one language, shared the same civilisation, and had in common the same immortal literature.

And now, a son of Oxford or Cambridge in the old island feels himself at home, amongst his own people and fellow-students, when he is welcomed at Harvard of the new continent. We all have but one language, the tongue now spoken by 130,000,000 of civilised men; and we have the same literature, the noblest literature of the modern world. And so, when I was honoured with the invitation to address you, I bethought me I would speak to you of the rise of that literature which is our common heritage, which more than race, or institutions, or manners and habits, makes us all *one* — which is far the richest, the most continuous, the most virile evolution of human genius in the records of Christendom.

I call to mind also that this year is the millenary or thousandth anniversary of the death, in 901, of Alfred the West Saxon King,[1] who is undoubtedly the founder of a regular prose literature, as of so many other English institutions and ways. Could there be a fitter theme for an English man of letters in an American seat of learning? There was nothing insular about Alfred; he was not British; he was not feudal; his memory is not stained by any crime done in the struggles of nation, politics, or religion. He lived ages before "Great Britain" was invented, mainly, I believe, in order to humour our Scotch brother-citizens; ages before Protestantism divided Christendom; ages before kingship ceased to be useful and republics began to be normal. Alfred was never King of England: he lived and died King of the West Saxons, the ancestral head of a Saxon clan. He and his people were just as much your ancestors as they were mine, for all we can say is, that the 130,000,000 who speak our Anglo-Saxon tongue have all a fairly equal claim to look on him as the heroic leader of our remote forefathers.[2]

---

[1] The year 901 is accepted by historians as the date of Alfred's death. Recent research by competent paleographers has made it more probable that he died in 899 or 900. See articles and letters in the *English Historical Review*, *Athenæum*, etc. The Millenary Commemoration Committee decided not to enter on the debated problem, but to adhere to the date generally recognised when the committee was formed.

[2] A large representative committee, of which the King is patron, was formed in 1898 to commemorate the thousandth anniversary of Alfred's death. A grand colos-

But I wish now to speak of Alfred not as our father in blood, or in nation, but as the real father of native prose, that common inheritance of us all, which, after a thousand years of fertility, has lost none of its vigour, its purity, and its wealth. The thousandth anniversary of his death has aroused new attention to his work, and has produced some important books to which I will direct your notice. Of Alfred the man, the warrior, the statesman, the hero, the saint, I will not now speak. In each of these characters he was perfect, — the purest, grandest, most heroic soul that ever sprang from our race. It is only of Alfred the writer of books, the creator of Saxon prose, that I wish to speak. He was indeed one of those rare rulers of men who trust to the book as much as to the sword, who value the school more than the court, who believe in no force but the force of thought and of truth.

In that noble and pathetic preface to his *Pastoral Care*, Alfred himself has told us how and why he carried through the restoration of learning in his church and people. When the first long struggle with the Danes was over, he found his kingdom desolate, and ignorance universal. There was not one, he says, on this side of Humber who could understand their mass-book or put a letter from Latin into Eng-

---

sal statue by Mr. Hamo Thorneycroft, R.A., is now being raised at Winchester, where he lived and died, by British and American subscribers. The Hon. Secretary of the English committee is Mr. Alfred Bowker, Mayor of Winchester. The Hon. Treasurer is Lord Avebury, of Robarts, Lubbock & Co., Lombard Street, London.

lish. He groaned to think how learning had flourished before the great invasion. He wondered how the good and wise men of old had omitted to translate their Latin books into English, so that the people might read them and hear them read. He supposes they could not believe that learning would die down so utterly. And so the great King set himself to work with all the fire of one who was both hero and genius to the twofold task, first, to restore learning and found a national education, and secondly to put the great books of the world into the mother-tongue of his people. For the first, he gathered round him scholars from all parts, without distinction of country or race, Welsh, Celts, Mercians, Flemings, Westphalians, as well as men of Wessex and Kent. The second task he undertook himself. Having mastered Latin late in manhood after strenuous toil, he became the first of translators, and in so doing he founded a prose literature.

As a boy, Alfred had shown his zest for study. He had been taken to Rome and to the Court of the Frank King.[1] But from the age of eighteen he was occupied for twenty years with desperate wars and the reorganisation of his kingdom. It was not until he had been king sixteen years, and was thirty-eight years old, that he found himself free for literary work. That he did all this, as he tells us with stately

[1] I incline to think that when Ethelwulf sent the boy to Rome at the age of four, Alfred remained there for perhaps over two years till his father brought him back; and, though he did not learn to read, his childish mind was filled with what he there heard of antiquity and of the Christian world. The fact that his name appears in charters when he was five does not convince me.

pathos, "in the various and manifold worldly cares that oft troubled him both in mind and in body," is to me one of the most mysterious tales of intellectual passion in the history of human thought. It places him in the rare rank of those warriors and rulers who, amidst all the battle of their lives, have left the world imperishable works of their own composition, such as did David, Julius Cæsar, and Marcus Aurelius.[1]

The works of Alfred are numerous, important, and admirably chosen.[2] His *Handbook* — a sort of anthology or golden treasury of fine thoughts which he collected whilst Asser was reading to him and teaching him to translate — has utterly perished, though William of Malmesbury, two centuries later, used and cited it. Ah! how many libraries of volumes would we willingly lose to-day if time would give up to us from its Lethean maw that well-thumbed book, "about the size of a Psalter," that the holy king was wont to keep in his bosom: the book wherein from day to day he noted down in English some great thought that had impressed him in his studies.

---

[1] See Pauli. *Life of Alfred the Great*, 1851, translated by B. Thorpe, Bohn's Ecclesiastical Library, 1857, with text and translation of the *Orosius*; also the Jubilee Edition of *Alfred's Works*, 1852–1853. The latest account of Alfred's career as king, warrior, lawgiver, scholar, and author is to be found in the volume published by the Alfred Commemoration Committee. *Alfred the Great* (Adam and Charles Black), London, 1899. 8vo.

[2] For the writings of King Alfred, consult the work just referred to and the essays therein of the Bishop of Bristol, and Rev. Professor Earle; also see Mr. Stopford Brooke's *English Literature to the Norman Conquest*. Macmillan & Co., 1898. 8vo. Chapter xiv, and R. P. Wülker's *Grundriss sur Geschichte der Angelsächsischen Litteratur*.

After his personal *Handbook* of thoughts came Alfred's *Laws*,[1] which we possess intact in several versions. This book for literary purposes is interesting only by its preface, evidently dictated by the King himself. Here we have in a sentence that spirit of order, of simplicity, of modesty, of self-control, of respect for public opinion, of reverence for the past time, and of solemn consideration of the times to come, which stamps the whole career of Alfred as ruler.

"I, Alfred the King, gathered these laws together and ordered many to be written which our forefathers held, such as I approved; and many which I approved not I rejected, and had other ordinances enacted with the counsel of my Witan; for I dared not venture to set much of my own upon the Statute-book, for I knew not what might be approved by those who should come after us. But such ordinances as I found, either in the time of my kinsman Ina, or of Offa, King of the Mercians, or of Ethelberht, who first received baptism in England — such as seemed to me rightest I have collected here, and the rest I have let drop. I, then, Alfred, King of the West Saxons, showed these laws to all my Witan, and they then said that they all approved of them as proper to be holden."

There spoke the soul of the true conservative, moderate, and far-seeing chief of a free people, a creator of states, such as were Solon and Servius in antiquity; such as were, in later days, some adored chief of a free people, a William the Silent, or a George Washington.

The books of which Alfred is certainly and strictly

---

[1] Dr. Felix Liebermann's *Gesetze der Angelsächsen*, 1898, etc. 4to. The latest critical edition of the Saxon laws; also see the essay, in the joint volume, by Professor Sir Frederick Pollock.

the author are five in number; all translations or adaptations from the Latin, and all typical works of standard authority. They were evidently selected with a broad and discerning judgment. Alfred's mind was essentially historic and cosmopolitan. So he began with the standard text-book of general history, the work of St. Augustine's disciple and colleague, Orosius, of the fifth century. Alfred again was preëminently the patriot — the *parens patriæ*. And accordingly he chose the *History of the Church in England*, or rather the Christian history of the Anglo-Saxon federation, by the Venerable Bede, to give his people the annals of their own ancestors. Alfred again felt a prime need of restoring the church in knowledge and in zeal. And so he translated the famous *Pastoral Care* of Gregory the Great — the accepted manual for training to the priestly office. A second work of Pope Gregory which he translated was the *Dialogues*, a collection of popular tales. Lastly, came the translation, paraphrase, or recasting of Boethius's *Consolation of Philosophy* — far the most original and important of all Alfred's writings. He thus provided (1) a history of the world, (2) a history of his own country, (3) a text-book of education of the priesthood, (4) a people's story book, (5) moral and religious meditations. I will speak of each of these, but principally of the last, the *Boethius*, which, by its originality and its beauty, gives us far the truest insight into the inner faith and the literary genius of the King.

There were some other works in which his impulse

is seen, but where his actual hand is not certainly to be proved. First and foremost comes the *Saxon Chronicle*,[1] the most authentic and important record of its youth which any modern nation possesses. During the active life of Alfred this yearly record of events is undoubtedly of contemporaneous authorship; and for the most important years of Alfred's reign it is very full and keenly interesting. The evidence is conclusive that the King gave the most powerful stimulus to the compilation of the record, and thus was the founder of a systematic history of our country; for we may truly say that no error of the least importance has ever been proven against the *Chronicle*, which is properly regarded as the touchstone of historic veracity to which all other annals are submitted. It is to my judgment clear that the history of the wars with the Danes as told in the *Chronicle* was prepared under the personal direction of the chief himself, if it was not actually dictated by his lips.

The King is said to have begun a translation of the *Psalms* of David, which was cut short by his death; but of these we have no known copy. The *Soliloquies* of St. Augustine[2] is of his age, and has been imputed to his authorship. I incline to the belief that the preface is his own work, and that he superintended, if he did not execute, the translation. The same may

---

[1] *Saxon Chronicle.* Text of all manuscripts and translation by B. Thorpe. Rolls Series, 1861.

[2] *Soliloquies of St. Augustine.* Text in *The Shrine*, by Rev. T. Oswald Cockayne, 1864–1870. 8vo.

be the truth of the *Book of Martyrs*.[1] Lastly, there is the King's *Testament*, which, though highly interesting, is hardly a literary composition. No one accepts the authenticity of the *Proverbs of Alfred*, composed some centuries later, nor do we attribute to him the translation of the *Fables of Æsop*, nor the treatise on Falconry. But these and some other works that are ascribed to him testify to the belief of ages long after his death that his literary activity was of wide range and of permanent value.

After studying the arguments of the Anglo-Saxon scholars about the order of time in the composition of these works, I incline to the view of Mr. Stopford Brooke in his *History of English Literature to the Norman Conquest, 1898*. He makes the order this,— the *Pastoral Care*, the *Bede*, the *Orosius*, and lastly the *Boethius*. This, at least, is the order I shall adopt; and it certainly lends itself best to the literary estimate. Most authorities put the *Boethius* earlier. But we must not rely too exclusively on paleography and dialectic variations in this matter. Paleographists and the dialect experts wage incessantly their own civil wars, and I am not always ready to swear fealty to the victor or the survivor of the hour.[2] A consensus of paleographists and experts in dialect is conclusive, or conclusive as far as it goes. But until we know all the circumstances under which a given manuscript was written, I am not prepared to surrender my own

---

[1] *Book of Martyrs*. Text in *The Shrine*.
[2] Wülker (*op. cit.*) gives a table of these differences amongst the editors.

common sense. There is a historical and a literary *flair* in these things, which ought not to be lightly distrusted, unless contradicted by indisputable written proof. We have no reason to suppose that Alfred wrote much, or even at all, with his own hand. Most great men of action dictate, and do not hold the pen. And the fact that a given manuscript has traces of a Mercian or a Northumbrian dialect is no sufficient proof that it could not be Alfred's work, unless we can prove that no Mercian, no Northumbrian, ever copied a book which Alfred had dictated, composed, or directed to be written.

The naïf and pathetic preface to the *Pastoral Care*[1] of Pope Gregory the Great is unquestionably the King's own work, and is a touching revelation of his intense love for his native land and his passion to give his people a higher education. I cannot read that simple outpouring of soul by the great reformer without seeing the confession that it was a most urgent task, and his own first attempt at translating; and thus I judge it to come next after his *Handbook* and his *Laws*. It was natural that a great and systematic restorer of learning should begin with the training of those who were to teach. And thus Alfred's first great literary work was the translation of the standard manual for the education of the clergy and of other scholars. He would often meditate, he says, what wise men, what happy times there were of old in

---

[1] *Cura Pastoralis*. Text and translation, edited by H. Sweet. Early English Text Society, 1871. 8vo. For the preface, see Stopford Brooke, *op. cit.*, p. 24.

England, how kings preserved peace, morality, and order at home, and enlarged their borders without, how foreigners came to the land in search of wisdom and instruction. Now, he groans out, all is changed, and in these days of war and distress hardly a man could read a Latin book. And yet, he adds, what punishments would come upon us if we neither loved wisdom nor suffered other men to obtain it: we should love the name only of Christian, and very few of the virtues. Then he goes on to speak of the ravages and burnings of the Danes, how the few books left were in Latin, and how few Englishmen could read that tongue. "Therefore," he says, "it seems better to me to translate some books, which are most needful for all men to know, into the language which we can all understand. And this I would have you do, if we can preserve peace, to set all the youth now in England of free men, whose circumstances enable them to devote themselves to it, to learn as long as they are not old enough for other occupations, until they are well able to read English writing." Here was a scheme of primary education for the people, education which was not made effective in our country until my own lifetime. And then he goes on to the higher education, ordaining that "those be afterwards taught more in the Latin language who are to continue learning and be promoted to a higher rank." Next, he tells us how he began "among other various and manifold troubles of this kingdom to translate into English the book which is called in Latin *Pastoralis*, and in English *Shepherd's Book*, sometimes word for word, and sometimes according to the sense, as I had learnt it from Plegmund, my Archbishop, and Asser, my bishop, and Grimbold, my mass-priest, and John, my mass-priest. And when I had learnt it, as I could best understand it, and as I could most clearly interpret it, I translated it into English; and I will send a copy to every bishopric in my kingdom."

Here, then, is a great ruler, more than a thousand years ago, when the area and population of his own country were far below those of a state of the Union, when their very existence was at stake, and they were surrounded by ferocious invaders, who designs a scheme for primary and superior education, and restores the church and the schools. Here is the man who began, and certainly had he been longer lived and enjoyed peace, might have carried through, the translation of the Bible, seven centuries before it was actually accomplished. There is a most fascinating relic connected with this very work. The Bodleian Library at Oxford possesses the very copy which the King sent to Worcester. It is inscribed Ðeos Bôc Sceal To Wiogara Ceastre, *i.e. This book shall (go) to Worcester*.[1] I saw it when I was last in Oxford. And when I took in my own hands the very copy of his toil which Alfred a thousand years ago sent with his greeting to his Bishop at Worcester, which he solemnly commanded in the name of God no man should remove from the Minster; when I held in my hand in the Ashmolean

---

[1] Bodleian Library. Manuscripts. Hatton, 20.

Museum[1] the very jewel which the King had made for himself (perhaps to bear upon his sceptre) inscribed, — *Ælfred had me worked*, — I felt something of that thrill which men of old felt when they kissed a fragment of the true cross, or which the Romans felt when they saluted the Sibylline books. If to-day we fall short in the power of mystical imagination, our saner relic-worship is founded upon history, scholarship, and jealous searching into the minutest footprints of the past.

Of the *Dialogues* of Gregory, we need say little, for the translation as yet exists only in three manuscripts. But I follow the view of Professor Earle, that the book is the King's work, as the characteristic preface most obviously is.[2] " I, Alfred," it runs, " by the grace of God, dignified with the honour of royalty, have understood and have often heard from reading holy books that we to whom God hath given so much eminence of worldly distinction, have peculiar need at times to humble and subdue our minds to the divine and spiritual law, in the midst of this earthly anxiety : " . . . " that I may now and then contemplate the heavenly things in the midst of these earthly troubles."

In the *Pastoral Care* the King carefully followed the text of the Latin, neither adding nor omitting anything in a revered book of such authority by the spiritual founder of Saxon Christianity. And in a first essay he proceeded with scrupulous attention to his

---

[1] Now deposited in the Taylor Museum, Oxford, and described in a new work by Professor Earle — *The Alfred Jewel, an Historical Essay.* 1901. Clarendon Press. Cr. 8vo. [2] Professor Earle's essay in joint volume, p. 198.

original. As he advanced in scholarship and literary skill, he became much more free, until in the *Boethius* he uses the Latin almost as a text for his own meditations. In the translation of Bede's *Ecclesiastical History*,[1] Alfred omits many sections, of which he gives a list; but he adds nothing, although there were many points as to the history of Wessex wherein he might have corrected and supplemented Bede's meagre statements. The translation keeps fairly well to the original, but it has no special literary value. The next translation of the King was the *History of the World* by Orosius,[2] which St. Augustine suggested as a companion to his own argument, in the *City of God*, that the wars and desolation of the Roman world were not caused by the spread of the Gospel. It was the only book known in the Middle Ages as a universal history, and it was as such that Alfred put it forth. But, as his object was essentially to educate, he adds full explanations of matters which Saxons would not easily follow, and his very elaborate additions on geography, the topography of the German peoples, the account of the Baltic and Scandinavia by the Norseman, Ohthere, have a freshness, a distinctness, and precision which peculiarly stamp the organising and eager grasp of a born explorer, who believed with the Prophet—"many shall run to and fro, and knowledge shall be increased."

---

[1] Bæda's *Ecclesiastical History*. Text and modern English, by T. Miller (E. E. Text Society), 1890–1898.
[2] *Orosius*. Text and Latin by H. Sweet (E. E. Text Society), and also by Thorpe, in Pauli's *Life*, translated. See Note 1, p. 75.

We come now to Alfred's *Boethius*, far the most important work of his pen. It is almost an original treatise, so great are the variations, additions to, and omissions from the Latin text. Whole chapters are dropped by the translator, and page after page of new thoughts are inserted. Some idea of the extent of this paraphrasing may be got, when we find the first *twelve* pages of the Latin compressed into *two* of Alfred's, and nearly the whole of the last book of the Latin, occupying fifteen octavo pages, dropped altogether, and new matter of the King's, filling nine pages, inserted. Alfred took the *Meditations* of Boethius as a standard text-book of moral and religious thought, and he uses it as the basis of his own musings upon man, the world, and God. Alfred intends his book to be for the edification of his own people. And, accordingly, he drops most of the classical philosophy; expands and explains the mythological and poetic allusions; and changes the Platonic theism of Boethius into Biblical and Christian divinity. The transformation is astonishing. As we read the Latin we find it difficult to understand why a book so abstract, and in places so metaphysical and technical, held the world of European culture for a thousand years down to the age of Shakespeare. But, when we turn to Alfred's piece, we are in the world of those poignant searchings of heart which pervade the *Psalms* of David, the *Imitation of Christ*, and the devotional books of Jeremy Taylor.

The millenary commemoration of the King has

drawn fresh attention both to Boethius and to Alfred's translation, and we may say that it is only in recent years that we have had adequate studies of both. Dr. Hodgkin's *Italy and her Invaders* and Mr. Stewart's excellent volume on *Boethius*[1] have collected in convenient form almost everything that is known about the Roman philosopher. And quite lately Mr. Sedgefield, of Melbourne and Cambridge universities, has published two books on Alfred's version: the first, a critical edition of the Anglo-Saxon text from the manuscript with a Glossary, the second a version in modern English prose, and an alliterative version of the metres.[2] Both the text and the modern rendering by Mr. Sedgefield are an immense improvement both in accuracy, scholarship, and elegance on the earlier editions whether of the old or the new versions. And it is only now, by Mr. Sedgefield's aid, and with the essays by the Bishop of Bristol and Professor Earle in the recent volume *Alfred the Great*, 1899, edited by the Hon. Secretary of the Millenary Commemoration Committee, and with Mr. Stopford Brooke's excellent chapter in his book already cited, that the real power of Alfred's work can be fully understood by the general reader.

This is not the occasion to enlarge on the story of

[1] *Italy and her Invaders*, by Dr. T. Hodgkin, second edition, 1896. Vol. III, chap. xii. Oxford University Press. *Boethius*. An essay by Hugh Fraser Stewart, 1891. 8vo.

[2] *King Alfred's Old English Version of Boethius de Consolatione Philosophiæ*, by Walter J. Sedgefield, Oxford University Press, 1899, and *King Alfred's Version of the Consolations of Boethius, done into Modern English*, by the same. Oxford University Press, 1900.

Boethius himself, or the strange fortune of his famous book. Dr. Hodgkin has given good reason to think that his political career was not one of such perfect loyalty and wisdom. And, if Alfred's introduction and zealous defence of him contains, as is probable, the church tradition about his life and death, Theodoric might fairly regard him as an enemy and a traitor. The King tells us that Boethius cast about within himself how he might wrest the sovereignty from the unrighteous King of the Goths, and that he sent word privily to the Cæsar at Constantinople to help the Romans back to their Christian faith and their old laws.

If Theodoric had grounds to believe that Boethius was really taking part in a conspiracy to urge the Eastern emperor to do what, in the next generation, Justinian did when he destroyed the Gothic kingdom in Italy, he would naturally treat the great Roman chief of the senate as a conspirator. It is not so improbable that the story, which Alfred may have heard at Rome itself not more than three hundred years after the fall of the Gothic kingdom, and which he treats as ample justification of Boethius, was the true story, or, if greatly exaggerated, still having a substantial basis in fact. If so, Theodoric did not suddenly become a ferocious tyrant; and St. Severinus, as Boethius was called in the church, lost his life and liberty in an abortive and very dangerous clerical conspiracy to destroy the Goths and restore Italy to the Greek empire.

But the special point to which I wish to call your

attention is the literary beauty of Alfred's own work. I estimate that about one-quarter of the whole book is original matter and not translation. There are seldom two consecutive pages in which new matter does not occur; and there are nine consecutive pages, in Mr. Sedgefield's editions both of the Saxon and the modern English, which are Alfred's original, so that we are well able to judge both matter and form of the King's work. Indeed, the *Consolations* of Alfred differ from that of Boethius as much as the *Confessions* of St. Augustine differ from the ethical Treatises of Seneca.

The *Consolation of Philosophy* seems to have had a curious attraction for translators in many languages. Mr. Stewart (in his sixth chapter) has given an interesting account of a great many of these, both English and foreign. The list of them fills many pages in the British Museum Catalogue. Mr. Sedgefield gives a long account of English translations in prose and verse, beginning with Chaucer, just five hundred years after Alfred, and continuing down to that of H. R. James in 1897. In all, Mr. Sedgefield gives specimens of no less than fourteen versions, from Chaucer to the present day, of which five are in prose. The most interesting of these versions are the two in prose: one by Chaucer at the end of the fourteenth century, one by our Queen Elizabeth at the end of the sixteenth century. We have thus ample opportunity for comparing the work of Alfred with that of other translators in the course of no less than five centuries. And I cannot withhold my own deliberate conviction that, as prose literature, the version of Alfred, in its simplicity, dignity, and power, is a finer type than any of the successors.

This is truly wonderful when we remember that the first translation is that of our great poet, Geoffrey Chaucer. But poets do not always write fine prose; and in the fourteenth century English prose was in a conglomerate and formless state. I will illustrate this by one or two instances, setting Alfred's prose beside that of Chaucer. Of course, to make myself intelligible, I shall transliterate Alfred's Anglo-Saxon into current English, using Mr. Sedgefield's admirable version. But this version is not really a translation. It follows the words of Alfred punctiliously, often changing nothing or little in the order, and removing little but the terminals and archaic forms of the words. This is transliteration, but not translation. I need not go into the question whether Alfred's Anglo-Saxon is English. He calls it English, and in spite of differences of construction, syntax, grammar, and vocables, it is the basis of English: perhaps two-thirds of it closely akin to some English dialects as spoken within a few centuries ago. The fact that the ordinary English reader cannot read a line of it, is not conclusive. He cannot read a line of Layamon's *Brut* or the *Ancren Riwle*,[1] both about a century and a half after the Conquest; nor indeed could he read a paragraph written phonetically in pure Scottish or Yorkshire dialect.

---

[1] *Specimens of Early English*, by Morris & Skeat. Oxford University Press.

I shall not enter on the question whether Alfred is the founder of *English* prose. Alfred certainly wrote or dictated a fine, organic, rhythmical prose in the mother-tongue used by himself and his people in the southwest and centre of England. Three-fourths of the words in that tongue survive in some altered form in English speech and its dialectic varieties. Whether it be the same language as English, depends on what we mean by that phrase. Grammar, syntax, pronunciation, have changed. The words mostly remain under modern disguises. I am not satisfied by the trenchant decision of Professor Marsh (*Origin and History of the English Language*). I prefer the views of Skeat, Morris, Earle, Green, and Stopford Brooke. I do not say as they do, that Alfred founded *English* prose. But in any case, he founded a prose in the language which is the basis of English.

I now give parallel passages from Alfred and from Chaucer. I take first Alfred's rendering of the fifth metre of Boethius's first book: the grand hymn — *O stelliferi conditor orbis*. Alfred's prose version is this, using always Mr. Sedgefield: —

"O thou Creator of heaven and earth, that rulest on the eternal throne, Thou that makest the heavens to turn in swift course, and the stars to obey Thee, and the sun with his shining beams to quench the darkness of black night: — (I omit four lines) Thou that givest short hours to the days of winter, and longer ones to those of summer, Thou that in harvest-tide with the strong North-east wind spoilest the trees of their leaves, and again in lenten-tide givest them fresh ones with the soft south-west winds, lo! all creatures do Thy will, and keep the ordinances of Thy commandments, save man only; he setteth Thee at naught." (Sedgefield, p. 5.)

Now here we have rhythm, force, dignity, and purity of phrase. This is fine literary prose — as Mr. Stewart well says, "his prose is informed with intensity and fire, and possesses all the vigour and swing of verse." Or, as Professor Earle says, it has "a very genuine elevation without strain or effort." It is true that in Mr. Sedgefield's English the order of words and the terminations are varied; but the original has to my ear the same fine roll:—

Eala thu scippend heofenes and eorthan, thu the on tha ecan setle ricsast, thu the on hroedum foerelde thone heofon ymbhweorfest, and tha tunglu thu gedest the gehyrsume.[1]

I now turn to Chaucer's[2] prose version of the same passage, modernising the orthography:—

"O thou maker of the wheel that beareth the stars, which that art fastened to thy perdurable chair, and turnest the heaven with a ravishing sway, and constrainest the stars to suffer thy law; so that the moon sometime shining with her full horns, meeting with all the beams of the sun, her brother, hideth the stars that be less; and sometime, when the moon, pale with her dark horns, approacheth the sun, loseth her lights: ... Thou restrainest the day by shorter dwelling, in the time of cold winter that maketh the leaves to fall.

---

[1] Sedgefield's *Anglo-Saxon* text, p. 10.
[2] *The Complete Works of Chaucer*, by W. W. Skeat, D.C.L. Seven volumes. 8vo. Oxford University Press, 1894–1897, Vol. II, p. 16.

Thou dividest the swift tides of the night, when the hot summer is come. Thy might attempereth the variant seasons of the year; so that Zephyrus, the debonair wind, bringeth again in the first summer season the leaves that the wind hight Boreas hath reft away in autumn, that is to say, in the last end of summer. There is nothing unbound from his old law, nor forsakes the work of his proper estate. O thou governour governing all things by certain end, why refusest thou only to govern the works of men by due manner."

Let us turn to the version of Queen Elizabeth, made exactly two centuries later: —

> " O framer of starry circle
>     who leaning to the lasting groundstone
>   With whirling blast heavens turnest
>     and Law compellst the skies to bear,
>   Now that with full horn,
>     meeting all her brother's flames
>   the lesser stars the moon dims
>     Now dark and pale her horn." [1]

But I cannot inflict on you any more of her Majesty's doggrel. She should have sent for Spenser or Shakespeare to help her, if she was bent on poetry.

Here is a specimen of the Queen's prose: —

"This, when with continual woe I had burst out, seeing her with mild countenance nothing moved by my moans: 'When thee,' quoth she, 'sad and wailing I saw, straight a wretch and exile I knew thee, but how far off thy banishment was, but that thou toldest, I knew not.'"

What a rigmarole in Queen's English! A question

---

[1] *Elizabeth's Boethius* (E. E. Text Society, 1899). Manuscripts Record Office, Domestic Elizabeth, 289.

may be asked — how can it be that the Saxon of Alfred in the ninth century can bear any comparison with the English of Chaucer in the fourteenth century, much less with the prose in the age of Shakespeare, Bacon, and Hooker in the sixteenth century? The answer I think is this. The old English of Alfred was a very simple, perfectly pure, and unmixed dialect of the great Gothic family of languages, of the Low-German class. It is homogeneous, with a limited vocabulary, using case endings like Latin, and not many prepositions. It was an easy instrument to wield, and a man of genius, nurtured in the poetry of centuries could at once become master of it. In the age of Chaucer, English had become much increased in its vocabulary; thousands of French and Latin words were being assimilated or tried; the structural form had been changed; and English prose was in a chaotic state, a state of solution. Chaucer's prose is immeasurably inferior to his verse. He did make a verse rendering of the fifth metre of Book II — *Felix nimium prior aetas*[1] which makes us long that he had translated Boethius's whole work into poetry, not into prose. Prose, as every one knows, is a plant of much slower growth than poetry. I am prepared to say it is more difficult, and in its highest flights a gift far more rare. And even in the age of Elizabeth, seven hundred years after Alfred, English prose was

[1] Given by Skeat in his *Chaucer*, Vol. I, p. 380. Slightly modernised it runs : —

"A blissful life, a peaceful and a sweet,
Ledden the peoples in a former age — "

only becoming perfectly organic in the hands of Hooker and Bacon.

But my purpose was not to make comparisons, but to direct attention to the dignity and beauty of Alfred's own thoughts. And for that end I will take a few passages which are Alfred's own, not translations from Boethius. Here is a bit from his introduction: —

"But cruel King Theodoric heard of these designs, and straightway commanded that Boethius be thrust into a dungeon and kept locked therein. Now, when this good man fell into so great straits, he waxed sore of mind, by so much the more that he had once known happier days. In the prison he could find no comfort; falling down, grovelling on his face, he lay sorrowing on the floor, in deep despair, and began to weep over himself, and to sing: and this was his song." (S. p. 2.)

What simple, pure, and rhythmical English, as formed and lucid as the English of Bunyan or of Defoe!

Another bit of Alfred's own, and what is so rare with him, a simile. Philosophy says: —

"When I rise aloft with these my servants (*i.e.* true wisdom and various skill) we look down upon the storms of this world, even as the eagle does when he soars in stormy weather above the clouds where no winds can harm him." (S. p. 2.)

Alfred is never more himself than when musing on his royal office: —

"Power is never a good thing, save its possessor be good, for, when power is beneficent, this is due to the man who wields it. Ye need not take thought for power nor endeavour after it, for if ye are only wise and good it will follow you, even though ye seek it not." (S. p. 35.)

What a magnificent Te Deum is this!

"One Creator there is without any doubt, and He is the ruler of heaven and earth and of all creatures, visible and invisible, even God Almighty. Him serve all things that serve, they that know Him and they that know Him not, they that know they are serving Him and they that know it not. He hath established unchanging habits and natures and likewise natural concord among all His creatures, even as He hath willed, and for as long as He hath willed; and they shall remain for ever." (S. p. 50.)

Hear how the head of the royal house of Cerdic, after some four centuries of kingly descent, speaks of nobility of birth:—

"Lo! all men had the like beginning, coming from one father and one mother, and they are still brought forth alike. Why then do ye men pride yourselves above others without cause for your high birth, seeing ye can find no man but is high-born, and all men are of like birth, if ye will but bethink you of their beginning and their Creator? True high birth is of the mind, not of the flesh; and every man that is given over to vices forsaketh his Creator, and his origin, and his birth, and loseth rank till he fall to low estate." (S. p. 75.)

Alfred takes small count of evil rulers. He says:—

"We see them seated on high seats; bright with many kinds of raiment, decked with belts and golden-hilted swords and war dress of many kinds. . . . But if thou wert to strip off his robes from such an one, and take away his company of retainers, then thou wouldst see that he is no more than any one of the courtiers who minister to him, if it be not some one of even lower degree." (S. p. 128.)

When we reach the grand prose hymn with which the book closes, I can find nothing more nobly expressed in the thousand years of English literature of which Alfred is the John the Baptist.

"To God all is present, both that which was before and that which is now, yea, and that which shall be after us; all is present to Him. His abundance never waxeth, nor doth it ever wane. He never calleth aught to mind, for He hath forgotten naught. He looketh for naught, pondereth naught, for He knoweth all. He seeketh nothing, for He hath lost nothing. He pursueth no creature, for none may flee from him; nor doth He dread aught, for none is more mighty than He, none is like unto Him. He is ever giving, yet He never waneth in aught. He is ever Almighty, for He ever willeth good and never evil. He needeth nothing. He is ever watching, never sleeping. He is ever equally beneficent. He is ever eternal, for the time never was when He was not, nor ever shall be. . . . Pray for what is right and needful for you, for He will not deny you. Hate evil, and flee from it. Love virtue and follow it. Whatsoever ye do is ever done before the Eternal and Almighty God; He seeth it all, and all He judges and will requite." (S. p. 174.)

I do not pretend to be a judge of sacred poetry; but I almost doubt if Dante, or À Kempis, or Milton have poured forth any psalm more truly in a devout spirit. I hold it to be in the way of pure and nervous English as fine as any similar outpouring in our language.

I do not touch on the difficult points in the Alfred manuscripts. These technicalities I leave to the experts. But I think the "experts" have been too positive in rejecting pieces on some very slight suggestion in orthography and dialect. From the literary point of view, I see no reason to deny the authenticity of the simple *Proem*, and still less of the noble *Prayer* which ends the *Consolations*. Both are to my mind instinct with the mother-wit, primeval simplicity, and God-fearing soul of the purest of kings, and the most spiritual of warriors and statesmen.

Nor need we discuss at length the vexed problem of the authenticity of the alliterative verses translating the poetry of Boethius, which are appended to the Cotton (Otho A. vi) manuscript. This has been treated mainly as a question of paleography and dialect; and the experts are divided and doubtful. I see no reason to doubt the conclusion of Mr. Stopford Brooke and of Mr. Sedgefield, that no good ground has yet been given to doubt that Alfred wrote the verse as well as the prose. The *Proem*, which I hold to be Alfred's dictation, distinctly says that after he had "turned the book from Latin into English prose he wrought it up once more into verse." The verse is not altogether poetry; it cannot compare with Beowulf and Caedmon. But to my ear it has the ring of Alfred's manly and native voice.

I will go on to say that even as verse these pieces do not seem to me quite so poor. Alfred, like many of us who love poetry, cannot compose poetry. And we do know some enthusiasts who persist in writing verses, when they know (or ought to know) that they cannot compose poetry. Alfred's verses seem to me the kind of lines that a great prose-writer, one who loved and studied poetry, but was not a born poet, might indite to occupy his hours of meditation. I confess I think there is a good ring in these lines: —

"Over Jove's mountain came many a Goth
Gorgèd with glory, greedy to wrestle
In fight with foemen. The banner flashing
Fluttered on the staff. Freely the heroes
All Italy over were eager to roam.

The wielders of bucklers, bearing onward
Even to Jove's mount far on to ocean
Where in mid sea-streams Sicily lieth,
That mighty island, far famed of lands."

(S. p. 178.)

Here is the metrical alliterative version of the grand prayer — *O stelliferi conditor Orbis* — of which we have just had the prose version: —

"O Thou Creator of bright constellations,
Of heaven and of earth; Thou on thy high-seat
Reignest eternal — Thou the round heaven
All swiftly rollest Thou by thy holy might
The lights of heaven causest to hear Thee."

(S. p. 182.)

I will not say that this is poetry; but it is, I think, as good as Sternhold and Hopkins's *Psalms of David*.

Here is a bit which has a touch of imagination in it — not entirely that of Boethius. The verse is more vivid: —

"Feather-wings have I  fleeter than a bird's
With which I may fly  far from the earth
Over the high roof  of the heaven above us;
But oh! that I might  thy mind furnish,
Thy inmost wit,  with these my wings,
Until thou mightest  on this world of mortals,
On all that there liveth  look down from on high."

(S. p. 222.)

Before I close, I will remind you of the judgment passed on Alfred's books by the accomplished historian of English literature — Mr. Stopford Brooke. "He was," he says, "the creator and then the father of English prose literature." His books "were the origin of English prose." The personal element, as he adds, stands forth clear in all his literary work. Mr. Stopford Brooke does not, I hold, quite do justice to Alfred's literary power as a translator when he says he had no creative power. Was not the translation of the Bible into English, yea, into German, perhaps into Latin also, a literary masterpiece, even though the translators inserted no new ideas of their own, or rather did not do so of malice aforethought? A great translation is a masterpiece; and two at least of Alfred's books are masterpieces in translation. But Mr. Stopford Brooke does full justice to Alfred's style as a writer. And to create the style of a new literature, to found the prose style of a nation, is a supreme literary triumph. Whether Alfred founded English prose style, is a question of the meaning of the phrase. Alfred, King of various tribes, then dwelling in England, composed in the vernacular a regular prose style not matched by any prose in England until the translators of the Psalms and Job, and in quiet force, simplicity, and purity not surpassed until the age of Addison.

We all know the often quoted, often misquoted phrase of Buffon, — *le style est l'homme même.* Of no one could this be said more truly — I venture to say so truly — as of Alfred. The whole range of ancient and modern literature contains nothing more genuine, more natural, more pellucid. He is not composing a book to be studied, admired, or criticised. He is baring his whole soul to us. He speaks as one on his knees, in the silence of his own chamber, in the presence of his God, who is pouring forth his inmost thoughts, hopes, and sorrows to the all-seeing eye, which knoweth the secrets of every heart, from whom nothing is hidden or unknown. And as he opens to us his own soul, as freely as he would bare it to his Maker, we look down into one of the purest, truest, bravest hearts that ever beat within a human frame.

And by virtue of his noble simplicity of nature, this warrior, this ruler, this hero achieved a literary feat; for he created a prose style five centuries before Chaucer, seven centuries before Shakespeare or Bacon, eight centuries before Addison or Defoe, and the full mastery of simple English prose. This in itself is a fact peculiarly rare in the history of any literature, where prose comes so much later than poetry. It can only be explained by remembering that the language which Alfred spoke and wrote was not exactly early English, nor middle English, much less that highly composite and tessellated mosaic we call the latest and contemporary English. It was but the bony skeleton of our English, what the Palatine mount of Romulus was to imperial Rome, what Wessex was to the present empire of the King. But it was the bones of our common tongue; it was the bones with the marrow in them, ready to be clothed in flesh and equipped with sinews and nerves. But this simple and unsophisticated tongue the genius of our Saxon hero so used and moulded that he founded a prose style, and taught the English race to trust to their own mother-tongue from the first; to be proud of it, to cultivate it, to record in it the deeds of their ancestors, and to hand it on as a national possession to their children. To this it is due (as Professor Earle so truly says) that "we alone of all European nations have a fine vernacular literature in the ninth and tenth and eleventh centuries," so that neither the French immigration, nor any other immigration has ever been able to swamp our English language. And when I say *We*, I do not mean *Britons*. I mean You of the Western Continent as much as us in the British islands. Alfred was as much your teacher, your ancestor, your hero, as he was ours. He spoke that tongue, he founded that literature, which is imperishable on both sides of the Atlantic, which is one of the chief glories of the human race, which the three corners of the world shall never be able to swamp by any immigration of any foreign speech — whilst we who are set to guard our common tongue, in the words of our great poet, to ourselves do rest but true.

# THE DUTCH REPUBLIC

# The Dutch Republic

ADDRESS AT COLUMBIA COLLEGE, NEW YORK, MARCH, 1901

SINCE the close of the Middle Ages four great peoples have succeeded in winning their freedom from civil and religious oppression, and have founded powerful and independent republics at the cost of their blood and a stormy revolution. These four were the people of Holland in the close of the sixteenth century, the people of England in the Civil Wars of the seventeenth century, and the people of the United States and of France in the second half of the eighteenth century. The revolutions of the Dutch and the Americans were primarily directed against foreign oppression; those of England and France were purely national uprisings which themselves ended in international oppression. All four revolutionary struggles, though separated by two centuries in time and by two hemispheres in space, had an intimate filiation of ideas with each other. All four, in different degrees, were at once both spiritual and political in aim, both intellectual and material in origin; and all four, in varying ways, tended to found a new conception of the social commonwealth.

I am now to speak of the Dutch Republic — the movement which, of all these four, was the earliest nearly by a century, founded a commonwealth that had far the longest duration; it was the movement which, of all the four, called forth the most magnificent display of heroism and endurance, which was victorious over the most terrific odds, which was (of the European movements, at any rate) the one least stained by anarchy, crimes, and horrors; a revolution which was organised by one of the purest heroes in modern history. Of all the chiefs who in the latter ages have led a free people against their oppressors we can count only Cromwell and Washington as worthy to rank in genius and in nobleness with William the Silent, Prince of Orange.

Not only was the struggle of the people of the Netherlands far the earliest, but it was also the most desperate and the most prolonged. Its first and most terrible bout was continued for some forty-two years from 1567 to 1609, and after an interval of twelve years it was again renewed from 1621 to 1648 — having been, with intervals, a war to the knife for more than eighty years. It was waged by a small and divided people against the most powerful monarch in Christendom, who hurled on them the most warlike soldiery in Europe, led by some of the most famous captains in modern history, and directed by some of the subtlest politicians of an age of experienced and sagacious statesmen. The petty province, hardly larger than a great English county, and not so populous, was for three generations assailed by all that war, famine, pillage, fire, torture, persecution, and inundation could do. It was deluged in turn with blood and with the salt sea — ruined first by exactions, then by confiscation, waste, destruction, and conflagration. And yet, after forty years of frightful suffering and heroic endurance in which old and young, men, women, and children, took equal share, the Dutch Republicans broke the power of Spain and swept her from their seas; and, after the second war of the seventeenth century, the States, by the Treaty of Munster (1648), humbled Spain in the dust, and were recognised as one of the greatest, richest, most aspiring Powers in Europe.

There is an often-quoted passage in a fine book — Voltaire's *Essai sur les Mœurs* — which is so brilliant and yet so truthful a summary of this great struggle, that I shall venture to quote it once more.

He says : —

" When we study the rise of the Dutch Republic, a state once hardly known, but one that in a brief space rose to a great height, we are struck by the fact that it was formed without design, and contrary to all that could have been expected. The revolution was begun by large and wealthy provinces of the mainland — Brabant, Flanders, and Hainault, — yet they did not shake off the tyrant. But a small corner of land, itself almost drowned by the sea, which subsisted only by its herring fishery, rose to be a formidable Power, held its own against Philip II, despoiled his successors of almost all their possessions in the East Indies — and ended by becoming their patrons and protectors."

This eloquent passage is a truthful picture of the great struggle which lasted with the interval I have stated for more than eighty years. I might occupy an evening in attempting to give you the history of any single one of these eighty years, and not one of them is wanting in thrilling interest. But my subject is simply the *Rise* of the Dutch Republic; and I shall understand by that the period comprised in Motley's work of this title which covers the twenty years or so from the beginning of the movement until the murder of the Prince of Orange in 1584. And I need hardly say that I can attempt to give you not the events of these crowded twenty years, but the main conclusions and problems. My subject, in fact, centres round the later life of " Father William," the founder of Dutch freedom and Dutch Protestantism.

To make my remarks intelligible, I will begin by a very brief outline of the principal events in the five and twenty years from 1559 to 1584. In 1506, Charles V of Spain, afterward the Emperor, succeeded to the inheritance of his ancestors, the Dukes of Burgundy — of all his vast possessions in the old and new world, the most thriving and industrious part. His famous abdication at Brussels in 1555 made his son, Philip II, King of Spain and Duke of Brabant, though of course not emperor as the empire was elective. For some four years Philip remained in the Provinces, carrying on a successful war with France, and vainly striving to crush the free burghers of the Low Countries into Spanish servitude and Catholic orthodoxy. Recognising his impotence, the sanguinary bigot withdrew to Spain to superintend auto-da-fés, furiously inveighing against the stubbornness of the Netherlands, and the machinations of their leader, the Prince of Orange. He was secretly planning a terrific vengeance and wholesale persecution.

After six years of veiled rebellion by the Flemings and irresolute oppression by the King's viceroys, Philip resolved to carry out the decrees of the Council of Trent, by all the horrors of the Spanish Inquisition, and shortly afterward armed insurrection begins. The monster Alva, one of the most consummate soldiers of his age, and a tyrant only second in ferocity and craft to Philip himself, was sent to the Provinces with a magnificent army of twenty thousand men,—Spanish, Italian and German. William withdraws before the storm into his ancestral countship of Nassau; Egmont and Horn are seized and executed; the Blood-Tribunal was set up; and a reign of terror by stake, axe, torture, fire and sword was established. For six years this raged unchecked. Eighteen thousand persons were put to death for religion; and twice or thrice that number were destroyed in battle, in sieges, or in general massacres. The armies of Alva and Alexander of Parma swept away the untrained burghers of Flanders and Holland, or the mutinous mercenaries whom the Nassaus hired in Germany. The patriot armies were massacred like sheep, city after city was stormed, and no sooner stormed but sacked with every form of ferocity, greed, and lust, and the whole population put to the sword.  Still they would not submit, and a new turn was given to the struggle by the Dutch of the Northern Provinces taking to the sea — "Water-Beggars," as they chose to call themselves.  They seized Briel, Flushing, and other ports in the low tide-swept islands commanding the great rivers as they pour into the German Ocean.  Louis of Nassau attacked the Spaniards in the South and in the end the Dutch asserted their hold on the provinces we now call Holland. Alva was succeeded by Requesens, Don John of Austria, and Alexander of Parma, the last, the ablest soldier of them all.  More defeats of the patriots followed, more cities were sacked and burnt, more provinces were desolated, and tens of thousands were massacred in cold blood.  All three brothers of William fell in the field ; he was left alone of all the nobles of the country in arms.  But slowly and steadily by sheer force of suffering and stubborn resistance, the Northern Provinces which we now call Holland won their virtual independence — in the grand words of the Roman poet : —

> "per damna, per caedes, ab ipso
> ducit opes animumque ferro."

Though defeated in every battle in the open field, the heroism of the defenders of Alkmaar, Haarlem, and Leyden equalled, if it did not surpass, the martial prowess of the Spanish veterans.  For a moment the whole seventeen provinces — we may call them roughly Holland and Belgium — were united.  But this

hollow union lasted but a few months, and about 1577,
after some ten or eleven years of struggle the Northern
Dutch Provinces were separated from the Southern
Belgian Provinces, and accepted William as their
chief. Steadily the vast power and military resources
of Spain recovered the Belgic Catholic population
which the House of Hapsburg retained until the end
of the last century. And as steadily the Dutch Provinces of the North grew in strength, wealth, and
patriotic energy. The union of Utrecht united the
seven Batavian Provinces in 1579, just twenty years
after the withdrawal of Philip, twenty years of frightful
suffering and heroic struggle. The Prince of Orange
was wisely, firmly, and impartially cementing this
Commonwealth into a hardy and rising State, when to
the horror of his own countrymen, and to the eternal
shame of all bigots and tyrants, he was foully murdered
by one of the paid assassins commissioned by the king
of Spain.

This tremendous struggle of more than eighty years
never would have been possible but for the foresight,
wisdom, and tenacity of William the Silent who may
be truly said to have founded a nation, even more than
Alfred created the English nation, as Washington
created the United States. The struggle was carried
on for more than sixty years after his death ; but, had
it not been for the desperate efforts he directed for the
first twenty years before, there would have been no
struggle at all. Philip would have annihilated the
feeble resistance of the Netherlands, divided by race,

religion, and local jealousies, and without leaders, resources, or any definite policy. William of Nassau and his family supplied leaders, a consistent policy, vast resources in money, and wide relations with Germany, France, and England. The Netherlands owed their salvation from a bloody tyranny to the heroic House of Nassau — and in a peculiar sense to the genius and indomitable will of the head of that house, William, Prince of Orange.

He had been trained from boyhood by Charles V, the Emperor, who regarded him as his adopted son, and the future mainstay of his own successor, Philip II. So soon as the Prince fully understood the nature and designs of the new king of Spain, he quietly but resolutely set himself to checkmate them. For six years, as general minister and counsellor of the Spanish government in the Netherlands, the Prince carried on a politic but outwardly loyal opposition to the tyrant's project of stamping out the new religion which, from North Germany, Geneva, and England, was making rapid progress, and of suppressing any show of local independence or right of taxation and representation. The efforts of William the Silent — who ought rather to be called William the politic, the persuasive, the affable — carried on the same work as did Hampden, Pym, and Cromwell in the early days of the contest with Charles I. And for some years he and his friends were entirely successful. And but for the fanatical violence of the Calvinists and their revolutionary outbreaks — and if Philip had been simply Duke of Brabant and Count of Holland, residing in Netherlands, and maintained by Flemish arms alone—there can be no doubt that William's scheme of founding a constitutional monarchy would have been crowned with an early and ample success.

Two things brought it to failure. The first was the furious temper of the Calvinist fanatics, and the fact that Philip was king of Spain, the most powerful monarch in Christendom, in command of boundless resources and the most brilliant soldiery known to modern history. The outbreak at Antwerp wrecking the noble cathedral, and the frenzy which carried similar outrages upon the religion of the State and of the majority, roused the Spanish nation, its king and the soldiers and nobles throughout his vast dominions to a passionate thirst for vengeance, which the Church excited to a white heat. Philip organised a magnificent army of some twenty thousand veteran troops, Spanish, Italian, and German, whom he despatched to Brussels to crush Protestantism and local liberty under the terrible Alva, one of the most pitiless and unscrupulous monsters of that age of perfidy and blood. Before this overwhelming power the Prince withdrew to his native Germany.

He withdrew but only to organise a desperate resistance.

For seventeen years he carried on the fight with the most marvellous energy, resource, and stubbornness—almost always defeated in the open field, pouring out the wealth of himself and his family like water, seeing one combination after another break up under the terror inspired by the Spanish arms, seeing one ally after another desert him, one foreign potentate after another play him false, and one brother after another slaughtered in fight. History presents hardly any other spectacle of dogged determination under incessant failure and defeat, and such versatility of resource in devising new plans after every failure and in organising fresh forces as each in succession was crushed or wiped out.

The marvellous ingenuity of these efforts was equalled only by the inexhaustible industry with which they were pursued. Some twenty or thirty volumes of very close print now reveal to us the endless schemes that for twenty years the Prince projected or matured. A mass of this correspondence exists in Mss. signed by William, or addressed to him. He seems to have spent hours almost daily in dictating despatches and secret instructions on every conceivable point. He had agents all over Germany, where his brothers and relations were powerful counts and officials, in France, all over the Netherlands, in England, even in Rome, and in the palaces of Philip, whose secret despatches were copied in his cabinet and sent off to the Prince. He held in his hand for twenty years the threads of numberless negotiations, plots, intrigues in many countries; he was constantly organising new levies, fresh campaigns, or local risings. And from hour to hour he had to decide a mass of details as to war, administration, diplomacy, religion, local disputes and suspicions.

It is in vain that we ask from William the Silent —
I prefer to call him William the Politic — that native
veracity of soul, that absolute transparency and rectitude of purpose which is so singularly rare in statesmen — which we find in Alfred, in St. Louis, in
George Washington — but perhaps in no other man
in supreme rule. Though William never sank to the
chicanery and mendacity of such men as Louis XI,
or Queen Elizabeth, or Mazarin, he was dark, secret,
and double-tongued even as at times were Richelieu,
Cromwell, Frederick, and Bismarck. He was no
spotless hero, no knight of romance, no mirror of
purity and truth. He was brought up in the worst
school of the worst age of Machiavellian craft; and,
though infinitely superior to the political schemers of
his age, he is no model of honour himself.

His true greatness was in his essential singleness of
purpose, — his unselfish devotion to a people which
was in no sense his own by birth, — in his resolute
rejection of dignity, power, or any kind of personal
gain, in his abhorrence of persecution and intolerance, and above all in his sublime constancy to the
cause to which he dedicated his life, his whole earthly
possessions, his peace, his family, and his good name,
and the unconquerable courage by which he held
to his purpose in spite of incessant defeat, and never
for an instant gave way to despair, though racked
with disease, deserted by all, and baffled a thousand
times in the long struggle by what looked to all men
an overwhelming power.

This heroic struggle of the Dutch to assert freedom of conscience and national independence, notwithstanding its narrow field, and, from a European point of view, its petty scale, exercised a decisive influence over the whole course of modern history. It was the first example in modern Europe of a small and poor country throwing off the weight of a foreign oppression and founding a free commonwealth on an enduring basis. Two centuries later its moral influence across the Atlantic, where a part of the American people were then of Dutch origin, is too obvious to be enlarged upon. But long before that, Holland had been the refuge of the oppressed, the home of freedom of thought, of Biblical religion, and of republican ideals. Its great service was to have instituted the duty of Toleration — in the spirit so nobly begun by William the Silent, and carried on by Barneveldt and De Witt, and Grotius. The relations of the Presbyterians of our own land with the Presbyterians of Holland were long and close; and many a victim of Stuart, Bourbon, and Papal tyranny found an asylum in the free republic. During the political and religious persecutions that for a century followed the Revocation of the edicts of Nantes by Louis XIV, the French Protestants and Reformers found a refuge in Holland. Descartes and Bayle lived and worked in Holland; and most of the unorthodox books which preceded the French Revolution profess on their title page to be published in Amsterdam. Thus, if the Dutch Republic was not politically associated with the Republic in France, from which it was separated in time by two centuries, so directly as it was associated with the Commonwealth in England and the Independence of the United States, its intellectual and moral influence as a type of freedom of conscience was very marked and decisive.

The Dutch Republic is not only the earliest example in modern Europe of the establishment of a free commonwealth,—we may put aside some petty cantons in mountain strongholds of mediæval origin, — but it has had the longest duration. The free government of Holland founded by William the Silent has now endured, we may say, for upwards of three centuries. It is true that his descendants for long periods held the hereditary office of Stadtholders; it is true that the Government of the United Provinces was not seldom arbitrary and oppressive. It is true that Holland has been now for eighty-eight years formally a kingdom. But it is still a free national government as completely as our own. Holland, for the 317 years since the murder of William of Orange, has been in the main a free, independent, and thriving State; and the charming young Queen, now in her twenty-first year, still rules the land created and saved by her great ancestor.

The struggle carried on by the people of Holland against all the might of Spain was for at least twenty years one of the most wonderful recorded in history. It may almost be compared to the defence of Greece against the myriads of Xerxes the great king. Philip II was absolute master of all Spain, of the Milanese, of Naples and Sicily, not to speak of his boundless possessions in the Indies from which streamed in for him incredible treasures in merchandise and gold. For the greater part of the struggle he held in stern subjection the great cities and rich provinces of Belgium. His Spanish infantry, his Italian cavalry and engineers were accounted the finest in the world. His footmen carried muskets, an arm till then almost unknown in Northern Europe. His generals and officers of every rank were consummate soldiers; in strategy, in tactics, in the mêlée, alike unsurpassed. Such captains as Alva, Don John of Austria, and Alexander of Parma were men of world-wide experience and true genius for war. Such an army as Alva led across Europe from Italy to Brussels on his terrible mission was an army perfect in every respect even from the point of view of modern war, — exact in discipline, duly proportioned in each arm, amply equipped, provided with officers of highest skill, and inspired by the grand munition of all armies, unbounded confidence in themselves and their leaders.

In spite of their ferocious conduct in the storm and their horrible duties as executioners, it is impossible not to be struck with wonder at the heroism of the Spanish infantry, at the impetuous valour of captains like Don Frederic, Vitelli, or Mondragon, who marched his men at night for miles through sea-water up to their shoulders, and then captured a fortress as they emerged from the sea. It is impossible not to admire the genius of Alexander Farnese, who in an hour and a half, with a few squadrons of cavalry and without loss, annihilated a brave army of twenty thousand men. Spain supplied the tyrant with dauntless warriors; Italy supplied him with consummate tacticians, administrators, and engineers; Germany and the Rhineland supplied him with willing mercenaries and soldiers of fortune; the Indies supplied him with inexhaustible gold, and Rome supplied him with the confiscations of heretics and the blessing of Heaven.

See the vast strength of the Spanish tyranny! Philip had not been three years on the throne of his father when he succeeded in humbling the whole power of France under her warlike King Henry II, by the brilliant victories of St. Quentin and Gravelines. A few years later his heroic half-brother, Don John, destroyed the magnificent navy of the Turks at Lepanto. And toward the close of his long reign he threatened England with the Armada — from which imminent peril we were saved by the skill of our seadogs and by a portentous tempest. That a despot of such vast resources, such splendid armies and mighty fleets, who seemed to his contemporaries, at least for some twenty years, to overshadow Europe and dominate the Western Continent, should have been defied, baffled, outmanœuvred, and eventually beaten by a poor and petty province, half of it salt marsh, inhabited by an unwarlike race of fishermen, and having no cities but a dozen or so of small towns, — this is a standing marvel of history. The only solution of the dilemma is the invincible power of courage, tenacity, a profound belief in a great cause, and the strength that lies in a man who is at once a hero and a genius.

The siege of Haarlem, which for seven months resisted a splendid army of Alva's, equal in number almost to the whole population of the town, is one of the great sieges in all history. Alva led against it thirty thousand of his veterans; the garrison was never more than a few thousand, with some hundreds of fighting women, regularly armed under the command of a widow lady of rank and good reputation. Twelve thousand of the Spaniards had fallen, after discharging ten thousand cannon shots upon the town, when starvation compelled the surrender. The whole garrison was butchered, and Philip thanked God and the Pope.

The siege of Alkmaar was quite as heroic and happily more successful, for Alva wrote to Philip, "I am resolved not to leave a single creature alive; the knife shall be put to every throat." His *gentleness* at Haarlem, he said, had led to no good result! At the first day's assault a thousand choice Spanish troops died in the trenches; men, women, and children of the besieged fighting on the ramparts with desperate fury. Under the orders of Orange the dykes were cut, and after nearly two months the besiegers withdrew in despair.

But the crowning triumph of all was the memorable defence of Leyden. That is indeed a story to stir the blood. Leyden is a town on the old Rhine, between

The Hague and Haarlem, one of the most ancient in Europe. Its memorable siege lasted, with a short interval, for a whole year, when it finally overcame the whole power of Philip. It was invested with sixty-two redoubts manned by some ten thousand troops under tried captains of Spain. The defenders were only the civilian burghers and a few irregular soldiers, behind imperfect and ancient walls. Their one chance was in William of Orange who was preparing a force to relieve them, and who adjured them to hold out for three months, which they swore to do. " As long as there is a living man left in the country," they said, " we will fight for our liberty and our religion." The city being by June strictly invested, the whole population was placed on a food allowance. Sorties and fierce combats took place daily. But the only chance of relief lay with the Prince of Orange who was entrenched near Delft, some twenty miles to the south, and was organising a fleet of small ships and barges. All prospect of meeting the Spanish armies on land was extinct. Louis and Henry of Nassau, brothers of the Prince, had but recently been defeated and killed in a great battle, with many of their friends and four thousand men, and the last chance of fighting the Spaniards in the open had been swept away. But the Prince, who had now lost three brothers in the struggle, would not despair. He tried another arm of defence — a new engine of war.

To understand this wonderful siege — wherein an inland city was succoured by seamen in a fleet, and a powerful army in a vast entrenched camp was driven off by discharging on them the sea from the German Ocean, we must have in our minds a picture of the spot. The whole country for fifty miles round is a huge plain, redeemed from the sea by centuries of labour, and lying many feet *below* the level of high tide, protected by vast dykes along the coast, and an intricate network of minor dykes inland, the whole intersected with thousands of canals and smaller channels, with sluices, gates, and dams innumerable. In this teeming plain rose, a few feet above the meadows, orchards, and woods, the graceful old city of Leyden, with a ruined tower on an artificial mound, by tradition said to date from the Romans or from our Saxon Hengist. The city was itself interlaced with canals — these were covered with hundreds of bridges of stone — and was protected by a range of ancient walls having huge gates and some antiquated towers and bastions.

The tremendous scheme of defence devised by the Prince, with the full assent of the city and the States, was to open the dykes that kept back the sea, flood the land for leagues, and across the drowned meadows, villages, and harvests, to send in to the doomed city the flotilla that he was organising with arms and food. It was the desperate resort of desperate men; for it meant the ruin of their homes and their lands for a generation. But they chose this — or death — rather than the Inquisition of Spain.

On the third of August the Prince in person superintended the cutting of sixteen dykes, and, waiting for the flood to rise, he had two hundred vessels laden with provisions. The waters rose slowly; and toward the end of the month the people of Leyden sent word that they were near to dying of hunger. "They had held out," they said, "for two months with food, according to promise, and then for another month, without food, but flesh and blood could stand it little more." The Prince replied that the dykes were cut and he was coming. But he was suddenly prostrated with fever, and lay in bed at Rotterdam in danger of death, very feeble, and almost speechless, but still dictating orders and sending messengers right and left.

By September Admiral Boisot, his chief officer at sea, came out of Zeeland with three hundred veteran sea-dogs, — wild, fierce men, half pirates, who were sworn neither to give nor to ask for quarter, — with inscriptions in their caps, "Better be for the Turk than for the Pope." With his fierce Zeelanders and some twenty-five hundred veteran seamen in large barges rowed with oars, and charged with cannon, arms, and provisions, Boisot pressed on across the flooded plain to within five miles of Leyden. There he was stopped by a huge barrier of dykes, whilst the Spanish army, three times as strong as his own, blocked the road between the dyke and the invested city. By the Prince's order the seamen assaulted and carried the dyke in a brilliant night attack, and at once, before the eyes of the enemy, cut a channel through the obstacle. Through it the little fleet poured, but only to find a second dyke, still a foot above the water, and guarded by Spaniards. This, too, Boisot carried — but even then he found himself barred by overwhelming numbers of the enemy. A strong east wind kept back the waters of the ocean and reduced the flood, so that the flotilla was aground. But gradually the besieging army was driven to narrower limits, and the villages round occupied and burnt by the seamen so as to give no shelter to the invaders.

Orange rose from his sick-bed, inspired the patriot army to fresh efforts, and ordered the cutting of the last dyke. The city was at its last gasp. All they knew of relief they had to guess from the roar of cannon and the blazing of villages in the distant country. Food had disappeared. Dogs, cats, and vermin were thought to be luxuries, starving creatures scrambled for offal and refuse in the gutters. Infants dropped dead from the dry breasts of their mothers, whole families were found lying dead in a house, for the plague appeared, and from six thousand to eight thousand died of it out of a population of fifty thousand. Still, men and women exhorted each other to endure — to resist the Spaniard and his priests — a fate more horrible than plague or famine. Some of the fainthearted ones did reproach the heroic burgomaster for his obstinacy, and placed a famished corpse against his door, as a mute witness to his cruelty. "Here is my sword," said he, "take it, kill me, divide me up, and eat my flesh — but no surrender whilst I live."

At the end of September a dove flew into the city with a message from Boisot; but the wind remained east, and the waters began to abate. But on the first of October a tremendous gale began from the southwest, forcing the sea over the plains, filling the canals, and carrying the fleet forward. Boisot was now right up to the entrenched works and the forts of the Spanish. Terrific day and night combats ensued, the sea rising steadily, the ships gaining ground, and the enemy sullenly retreating. On the night of the second of October, a combined assault on the Spanish lines was made by Boisot in his ships and by the men of Leyden in sortie. Caught between two fires, in the confusion of a pitch dark night, in the flood and roar of tempest, and stunned by the crash of a long section of the city wall that fell in the darkness, panic seized the enemy, and the Spanish general drew off the remnant of his splendid army, to such unflooded causeways and eminences as he could find: "beaten," wrote the proud Spaniard, "not by the enemy but by the sea!" This time Philip did not thank God — let us hope he did nothing worse.

On the morning of the third of October, a day ever memorable in the annals of Holland, — in the annals of heroism and patriotism, — Boisot swept into the city with his vessels, and the famished populations swarmed along the quays, the seamen throwing them bread as they rowed up the canals. The Admiral and his men, wild Zeelanders and all, burghers, women, and children, poured into the great church and offered up thanksgiving and sang a hymn. A message was sent to the Prince, which reached him, at Delft, also in church. He had it read to the congregation *after* the sermon, — should we all of us have had patience to sit out that sermon, with news of life and death to our people in the minister's hand? — but the Dutch are a patient and long-suffering race! The Prince set out to Leyden where he was received with enthusiasm. "It will cost Philip half his kingdom to make an end of us," he had said, and he had kept his word. He offered, in the name of the States, that as a reward for the sufferings and gallantry of the city, they might choose a remission of taxation or the foundation of a University, and the tradition is that Leyden chose the seat of learning, and rejected the filthy lucre. Should we to-day be capable of so noble a devotion to learning? But I believe the tradition to be mythical, and that Leyden was duly rewarded by a remission of taxes and also honoured by a seat of learning. Certain it is that the illustrious University of Leyden, the school of so many great teachers, of Grotius, Bœrhaave, and a crowd of men of science, of law, of theology, and of medicine, down to our day, was founded on this occasion, and is thus associated with the memorable siege — one of the most splendid triumphs of freedom and of constancy in the roll of history.

This tale of slaughter, ferocity, and heroism is only an *incident* in this long struggle. There were scores of sieges hardly less terrible, less gallant, though none of them so triumphant for the patriots. Whole provinces were desolated with fire and sword, pillage and flooding; armies were painfully mustered and equipped by William and his family, friends, and colleagues at the sacrifice of their entire fortunes, only to be swept into the rivers or hacked to pieces in a few hours by the matchless chivalry of Spain. Yet by sheer power to suffer and to endure, slowly the Northern sea-washed districts and the towns therein, which stood on piles a few feet above the waters around, won a precarious independence, began to form a solid confederacy, nay, rose into flourishing lands and even wealthy cities. How was it done? What was the secret? "'Tis dogged as does it!"— says an old navvy in a famous story. "Dogged"— it was— and also the magical resources of the *sea* by those who love the sea and know how to use the sea! The Southern, Catholic, Belgian Provinces and cities after incessant turmoil and bloodshed fell back into the grasp of Spain— step by step the Northern, Protestant, Dutch Provinces and cities asserted their liberty under their "Father William."

Let us try to picture to ourselves this "Father William," and see what manner of man he was. If anyone were to imagine him to be a dark, inscrutable, fanatical Puritan,— a sort of Calvinist Richelieu— a Protestant variety of Philip II,— he would indeed go wrong. William the Silent, the chief of the Dutch national revolution, the head of the Calvinistic Reformers of Holland, was neither taciturn by habit, nor a Dutchman by birth, nor a revolutionist in policy, nor an advanced reformer in religion. He was a most eloquent speaker, a delightful conversationalist, a brilliant man of the world, an accomplished linguist. He was by birth a Count of the Empire, a Nassauer, a German, of pure High German descent for long generations both by his father and his mother. Though Prince of Orange, which is on the Rhone in southeastern France, he never saw Orange in his life, and had little more to do with it than our Prince of Wales has to do with his own titular principality. William, Count of Nassau, got nothing out of Orange, except the barren honour of " Prince," and the degrading privilege of being addressed by Philip II as " my cousin." His princedom, his vast estates in the Low Countries, and his connection with Holland, he owed to accident in early youth. They came to him when a boy of eleven, in the lifetime of his own parents, under the will of his cousin René, of that elder branch of the Nassau house, settled in the Netherlands. From his boyhood William was thus all his life a sovereign prince; he was by instinct a real conservative, a moderate, a coalitionist — never a revolutionist. By policy he was an opportunist, always prone to take half a loaf, to get the best terms to be had at the time, to make the most workable compromise in each case.

His precocious apprenticeship in high matters of state and his wonderful insight into the nature of men he acquired by the favour of that consummate diplomatist, the Emperor Charles V, who made the young Prince of eleven his page, gave him the best education of the age, and kept him, almost as an adopted son, about his own person, even calling him to his side in his Cabinet whilst discussing affairs of moment. For nine years the young Prince was thus trained by one of the greatest masters of statecraft in an age of profound and ambitious politicians. At the age of eighteen, William was given in marriage by the Emperor to Anne of Egmont, one of the greatest heiresses of the Netherlands; and their joint possessions made them one of the wealthiest young couples in Northern Europe. The young soldier was shortly made a colonel and sent off to fight the French. He rose in the service; and at the age of twenty-two, the Emperor, himself one of the first soldiers of his age, made the young hero commander-in-chief of an army of twenty thousand men.

For some ten years the Prince continued to serve the Emperor, his son Philip II, and their successive viceroys in military and civil offices of the first rank. He took part in the successful wars against France that opened Philip's reign, though he does not appear to have done more than prove himself a consummate organiser of difficult campaigns, and a most wary and provident commander. It was when leaning on the shoulder of his beloved Prince, that the broken Emperor, in his theatrical scene of abdication, came into the Hall of Nobles to abdicate his crown into the hands of his own son, Philip. The dying sovereign leaned on the two Princes, his adopted and his natural son, those two who were destined to wage a deadly war against each other for nearly thirty years. For some years the Prince and his young bride kept royal state, as having a household renowned throughout Europe for its splendid hospitality, its brilliant refinement, and its magnificent courtesy. The Prince, wrote a bitter Catholic, has the most winning manners, the sweetest temper, the most persuasive tongue in the world. He leads all the court at his own will, and fascinates all he approaches, both high and low. He undertook at his own cost splendid embassies; he entertained all royal guests from foreign countries; he raised and maintained whole regiments in the field at his own charges, until even *his* vast revenues became encumbered with debt. Down to the age of thirty, William of Orange was in fact a grandee of the Spanish Crown, a magnificent Prince in four countries which are now France, Germany, Belgium, and Holland — and till then he was a devoted and indeed a loyal servant of the kings of Spain.

But he soon had a rude awakening from this prosperous pageantry. From the first day he had seen deep into the black heart of Philip, and though he felt in duty bound to serve him as a sovereign in the field and in council, he held him in deep aversion and distrust. Orange had a principal hand in the negotiations for the treaty of Cateau-Cambresis by which Philip so humbled his rival of France, and he was sent to Paris as a State hostage along with the Duke of Alva, the Prince's future foe, and Count Egmont, Alva's future victim. There, riding one day in a hunting expedition, alone beside the French king, Henry II, supposing the Prince to be deep in all the counsels of Philip, revealed to him the horrid plot concocted between Alva and the French court to combine to crush out the Reformation by all the rigour of the Inquisition, Philip to use his Spanish troops in the Netherlands. The Prince of Orange — he was still only twenty-six — never moved a muscle, but full of horror as he was, suffered the King to talk on. "I was deeply moved with pity," he wrote twenty years later, "for all the worthy people who were thus devoted to slaughter, and for the country to which I owed so much, wherein they designed to introduce an Inquisition more cruel than that of Spain. From that hour I resolved with my whole soul to drive the Spanish vermin from the land." He hastened to get leave of absence, returned to Brussels, saw some of his friends and warned them of what was to come. It was this incident which gained the title of "the Silent One" for a man who was one of the most eloquent talkers and one of the most affable companions of his age.

We know how the Prince looked at this time. There exists a fine portrait of him painted exactly at this age — a replica of which his descendant, the German Emperor, has recently presented to his own cousin, the young Queen of the Netherlands. The Prince is in full armour resting his left hand firmly on his helmet, with powerful features, an open brow, auburn hair, large piercing eyes, a very firm, strong jaw, a mouth closely set, and a massive chin. The whole aspect is one of intense penetration, firmness of purpose, and even then of deep melancholy. It is pathetic to contrast this picture of his resplendent youth with the portraits of his last years when, an old man at fifty-one, he was bald, worn with wrinkles and furrowed with disease and anguish. The mouth seems locked with iron, and the deep eyes are those of a man at bay fighting fiercely for life.

In religion, as in all things, the Prince was an opportunist, willing, in an age of a wild chaos of beliefs and the clash of sects, to accept the best working compromise in outward communion, whilst quietly holding his own beliefs and insisting on respect for those of others. He was a man of deeply religious feeling, and sincere natural piety, sprung of a religious family, who himself brought up his own family in practical godliness. But he seems never to have held to any dogmatic creed whatever. And in an age when creeds were all flung together into a melting pot, and when each sect in turn was doing deeds and uttering maledictions that dishonoured all their professions, William's own religious adhesions were singularly varied. He was born and baptized a Lutheran, his father and his mother being convinced Protestants. When adopted by Charles V at the age of eleven, he was brought up a Catholic, and he remained in conformity with the Catholic Church down to the age of thirty-four and his withdrawal into Germany. Then he was for a time in practical communion with the

Lutherans; and finally, when he became chief of the Northern States, and Stadtholder of Holland he lived and he died a Calvinist.

Throughout his life he had a loathing for the persecuting temper of Catholicism; Lutheranism seemed to him always to have too much of the aristocratic and political spirit; and he deeply distrusted the fanatical zealotry of Dutch Calvinism. He was always striving to create a *modus vivendi* between bitter partisans. As a great Catholic official, he laboured to protect the Reformers; as Lutheran, he laboured to induce them to help the Calvinists; as a Calvinist chief himself, he vehemently resisted their unchristian passion against all outside their own sect. William's whole life, from the day when he listened in horror to the infernal plot of the two kings until the day when he gasped out his last words, "My God, have pity on my soul and this poor people!" his whole life was a plea for toleration — mutual forbearance — Christian unity.

William had four wives, by whom he had thirteen children. His first wife, Anne of Egmont, was a Catholic, and she died young before the great struggle began. His second wife, Anne of Saxony, a Lutheran and daughter of the great Lutheran duke, was a violent Protestant, the Prince remaining Catholic, and baptizing her children in that Church. As she plunged into vice and crime he repudiated her. She was divorced, tried and condemned by law, and died mad in prison. His third wife, whom he married whilst the second was alive but divorced, was a Bourbon princess, an ex-abbess, a convert to Protestantism, and a refugee. It was a marriage that filled the French Court and the Catholic world with horror, a desperately imprudent step on the Prince's part. His fourth wife, Louise de Coligny, daughter of the heroic Admiral, had seen her father and her husband assassinated in the Saint Bartholomew, and was destined to see her second husband also assassinated before her eyes by the same ruthless enemies.

The Prince was an eminently domestic man, almost excessively uxorious, a second father to his widowed mother, affectionate to his wives, loving to his children, and the soul of kindness and courtesy to all within his household. Of the thirteen children, but three sons grew up to manhood. The eldest was kidnapped into Spain by Philip and died without issue. The second, Maurice, nobly carried on for forty years and completed the work of his father. The third son, Frederick Henry, was born in the year of his father's death, and ultimately succeeded Maurice, as Prince of Orange. It is curious to note how many famous rulers, soldiers, and royal persons have traced their descent to William of Orange. The Princes of Orange first, the elective or hereditary rulers of Holland from his day until ours, during more than three centuries — then of course the second great Prince of Orange, William III of Holland and King of England. Through daughters come the royal family of Prussia, Frederick the Great, and the reigning Emperor, the Electress Sophia of Hanover, and of course all our Hanoverian royal family, then the Orleans princes, many of the Italian princes, not to speak of Prince Rupert, Marshal Turenne, Alexandra, Queen of England, and the royal family of Denmark and the Czar of Russia. The ancestors of William of Nassau were illustrious for four or five centuries at his birth. But his descendants, in the three centuries since his death, have been even more profusely scattered upon the thrones or around the thrones of Europe.

Such was the man who for twenty years withstood the machinations, the armies, the assassins of Philip II — never despairing, never relaxing his vigilance, never driven into crime himself. He countermined the conspiracies of Spain by his own foresight and his system of spies; after every defeat he raised up a new army; driven out of one stronghold, he raised up another; after every act of treachery and disunion, he set himself indefatigably to piece together a fresh combination. His knowledge of men, his insight into all the windings of the subtlest human heart was intuitive; his patience, his equanimity, his urbanity were never shaken for an instant.

In the long struggle the Prince was deeply changed within and without from the chivalrous grandee of his youth. His enormous revenues had all been confiscated by the tyrant or sunk in war. But one brother survived; and he and the rest of the family had ruined themselves in the cause. Father William, the idol of his own Hollanders, looked and lived like the simplest of his people. A fine courtier of Elizabeth, who saw him at Delft in these latter days, said he wore a threadbare old gown that a poor student would have been ashamed of, and through it could be seen for waistcoat a rough bargee's jersey, and his company was that of the citizens of that beery town. No external sign of his degree could be seen, but on conversing with him, the dainty courtier remarks, "there was an outward passage of inward greatness."

It would have been strange if there had not been something to mark the greatest man of his century. His later life was one of endless toil and hardship and often of real penury. When Louise de Coligny came to be married from France, where she had known the most brilliant Court in Europe, the Prince of Orange sent to bring his bride an open country cart, in which she had to sit on a hard board and was cruelly jolted. The States assigned to him a small sequestered convent, and there he kept a simple and almost open house, absorbed in work, and accessible to all. The spot still stands unchanged. It is now a national memorial and museum, and was the scene of the last tragedy.

The monster Philip, finding all his efforts to crush the Prince in vain, issued, in 1580, by the advice of Cardinal Granvelle, his ban whereby he declared Orange the enemy of the human race — offered a reward of twenty thousand golden crowns for his head, and promised his assassin full pardon, and a patent of nobility for himself and his family. From that hour William was hunted by murderers. One, Jaureguy, succeeded in sending a bullet through his cheek and palate, severing an artery in the neck. His life was saved by a miracle, but his third wife died of the shock. William's only care was to call out to spare the assassin, and from his sick-bed he saved the accomplices from torture. We know of some five or six conspiracies, and doubtless there were as many more we do not know of. William, like Elizabeth of England, lived for four years surrounded by assassins; but, alas! he had no Burleigh, no Walsingham to protect him.

The end — the inevitable end — came at last. William was at table with his family and a friend or two in the Hall of the Prinzenhof at Delft, the old convent. He passed out to his cabinet, and in the dark corner of the staircase lay concealed a small fanatic who shot him through the chest point blank. The Prince sank into the arms of his family, gasping out the words I have cited before, "God help this poor people!" It was July, 1584. He still was but fifty-one — in the prime of his powers.

The old Prinzenhof, a convent of the fifteenth century, is now a relic of Dutch patriotism — a place of pilgrimage to their people and all who love the cause of liberty and conscience. The hall where the hero lay dying is now filled with portraits, arms, views, engravings, tapestries, chairs, and tables of the period, and memorials that record the great struggle. They profess to have kept the hole in the wall where the fatal bullet struck. That murderous shot filled with triumph and exultation the whole Papal, Jesuit, tyrannic world, and struck indignation and dismay into the patriots, and all friends of the Protestant and national cause. It struck them with dismay, but not with despair. The people of Holland and Maurice of Nassau, his son, took up the gage, and for thirty years more successfully carried on the fight. It was but a year or two ago since I was standing in the dark passage where the bloody deed was done. And then I stood in the ancient church beside the noble tomb of Father William, and his long line of descendants, chiefs of Holland, with his motto, "*I will maintain piety and justice.*" I felt how deeply the three centuries that have passed have taught us all that civilisation owes to the founders of the Dutch nation, and to their great hero, whose name and fame will last, I believe and trust, for thrice three centuries to come.

# RECENT BIOGRAPHIES OF CROMWELL

# Recent Biographies of Cromwell

### A Lecture given at Princeton University

THE tercentenary of Cromwell's birth, which occurred in April, 1899, aroused fresh interest in the life of the great Protector, and saw the official acceptance of his memory as one of the national glories of England. Lord Rosebery, in an address worthy of himself and of the occasion, rehearsed all that our country owes to the heroic chief of our Civil War, and set up at Westminster Hall the fine bronze statue of Cromwell, which as Prime Minister he had called on Parliament to vote. This is one of the most impressive monuments in London; and it is a curious illustration how "the whirligig of time brings in his revenges," that the effigy of the republican general is finally set up, after so long a struggle, beside the Palace of Westminster; almost at the portal of the Parliament House, which he once closed and so often opened; hard by the Hall where he was installed as Protector; and a few yards from the tomb in which he was laid by the nation and from which he was torn by an infamous king.

The commemoration also very naturally gave rise to a number of new lives and memoirs of Oliver, both

English and foreign; which, though they may have established nothing new, may be said to have finally settled the true place of Cromwell in the history of England. We have had no less than three works from Mr. Gardiner, whose whole life has been devoted to the history of this age. Mr. Firth, who has worked on the same period for many years, published last year his *Oliver Cromwell and the Rule of the Puritans in England*. Then Mr. John Morley, in the same year, published his most fascinating and suggestive estimate of this ever memorable time. Dr. Horton and Sir Richard Tangye had both published volumes of unqualified eulogy from the point of view of modern Protestantism. And in America we have had the elaborate history *Cromwell and His Times* by Samuel Harden Church, and the spirited study by Theodore Roosevelt, Vice-President of the United States.

These various estimates differ no doubt somewhat in degree, and they differ much more in literary merit and in independent research. But they all, from various points of view, come to the same result. They all reject or ignore the pure Carlylean gospel of the supreme Cromwell — an almost superhuman and quite infallible being, whom to doubt was blasphemy and whom to thwart was sin. And they all agree in regarding Cromwell, whatever his defects and his errors, as a statesman of profound genius and of noble character. Some of these writers are more severe on his faults and his failures, some are more ready to blame his contemporaries and to expatiate on his difficulties. But in the main they make his services and his merits far outweigh his failures and his shortcomings. The tercentenary commemoration which saw him installed again at Westminster Hall in bronze, has seen him definitely enthroned in English literature with a chorus of honour — *ære perennius* — as one of the noblest of our English heroes and one of the chief spirits of modern civilisation.

No one can speak of biographies of Cromwell without beginning with the voluminous works of Mr. Samuel Rawson Gardiner, himself one of the descendants from Oliver. Seldom in English literature has any student devoted himself for a period so long and with such indefatigable zeal to master every shred of written or printed material that any language or country retains, and to weld these materials into the annals of a single epoch. From the year 1603 down to the year 1656, that is, from the accession of James I to the third year of Cromwell's Protectorate, we now have, in seventeen massive volumes, Mr. Gardiner's history of England. Few periods of half a century have ever been recorded with such immense learning and scrupulous completeness. The "master historian of the seventeenth century," as Mr. Morley has named him, has raised a monument of erudition of which the only drawback is the difficulty it presents to the ordinary reader to find his way through so vast a mass of research, and the consequent loss of proportion from the multiplicity of detail.

But it is in the two biographical pieces rather than in his *history* that we best find Mr. Gardiner's estimate of the Protector. In the voluminous history we so often come upon the sneers and insinuations of foreign diplomatists, the failure of some scheme, or the result of some error of judgment, that we almost begin to think of Oliver as the sport of circumstance, and the vacillating leader of a capricious party. When Mr. Gardiner has to sum up his view of the genius and character of the Protector in a small volume, we there find a larger estimate and a broader standard. Mr. Gardiner, though he is no painter of character, nor master of vivid narrative, has an eminently judicial mind. And, when he is delivering judgment, we are bound to recognise the weight of his words. The fine monograph which he prepared for M. Goupil's splendid quarto is an excellent summary of Oliver's career. And the sentences in which he closes the volume may be taken as the general verdict of posterity: —

"The limitations on his nature — the one-sidedness of his religious zeal, the mistakes of his policy — are all thrust out of sight, and the nobility of his motives, the strength of character, the breadth of his intellect, force themselves on the minds of generations for which the objects for which he strove have been for the most part attained, though often in a different fashion from that in which he placed them before himself."

The six Oxford Lectures entitled *Cromwell's Place in History* (1897) give us a much more critical estimate. The sixth lecture recapitulates the whole. In it Mr. Gardiner tries to draw the distinction between *negative* and *positive* acts. "His negative work lasted," he says, "his positive work vanished away." No hard and fast line can be drawn between negative and positive acts of the soldier and the statesman; and it is misleading to attempt to distinguish negative from positive work. The French Revolution, the campaign of Waterloo, the defeat of the Confederate Rebellion by the United States, were peculiarly negative, — and yet, how fruitful in positive results! It would be a paradox to say that Mirabeau, Wellington, and Grant left behind them no positive effects. Finally, to shatter the ancient *régime*, the tyranny of imperialism, or the consolidation of slavery, were each achievements that led to vast and enduring changes in human societies. The task of Cromwell was of this order, and its negative or destructive side was quite as lasting and quite as much charged with new conditions as was that of these men. To destroy forever an effete political and social system is practically to found a new system. And Cromwell was the main instrument in destroying the effete political and social system identified with feudalism, the Stuart monarchy, and the Laudian church.

The Commonwealth and the Protectorate destroyed the Old Monarchy and the Feudal Constitution, and opened the way to our Liberal Institutions. Stuarts, intolerance, and corruption returned for a brief space, and in diminished force. England at the accession of Anne was wholly transformed from what England had been at the accession of Charles I. Monarchy, peerage, Parliament, law, justice, toleration, finance, commerce, religion, — all stood on a new footing. This immense transformation was not effected by Cromwell; but without him it would have been impossible. The Protectorate was followed by the Restoration, and most of its direct acts of State were annulled. Cromwell strove to found a presidential government, like that of the United States, rather than a parliamentary government, as understood by the Whigs. Our subsequent history was a compromise, and much of it was anti-Cromwellian. But it was Cromwell who, in the evolution of the English nation, made our subsequent history possible.

"There was no single act of the Protectorate that was not swept away at the Restoration without hope of revival," says Mr. Gardiner. This is to view the career of Cromwell from too close a point, and through too small a lens. Destructive work, in statesmanship, provided it be *permanent*, is *ipso facto* constructive, if it enables the new system to form and grow. Luther, Wickliffe, Latimer, were destructives in theology, as Voltaire, Hume, and Kant were destructive in metaphysics; but vast constructions have been built on the ground they cleared. Alexander, Julius Cæsar, Charles the Great, William the Silent, effected memorable works of reconstruction. Yet the institutions laboriously founded by each of these perished with them; and hardly one of them left anything absolutely permanent behind him, unless it were the city of Alexandria, the Julian Calendar, and the prestige of Charlemagne and of Orange. William the Silent's whole career was one of failure. Yet, after three centuries, the nation he created reveres him as its founder, and the British Empire is now fighting, in the Orange Free State, the scanty offshoot of that nation.

That destructive statesmanship should be constructive in result requires many important conditions. The destruction must be necessary and timely; it must be final; it must prepare a permanent reconstruction. The Protectorate fulfilled all these conditions. Although many of the Protector's schemes and arrangements disappeared with him and some of them before him, they were ultimately succeeded by institutions of a similar order and having a like purpose, which never could have been founded at all had not Cromwell's reforms and experiments preceded them. Like William the Silent, Cromwell failed at times because he was in advance of his age, especially in the matter of religious equality, official competence, law reform, and the proper spheres of Parliament and Executive. Had Cromwell had his way he would have made the political system of England akin to that of the United States. The parliamentary system of government was not established in England for more than a century after Cromwell's time. It is not at all clear that it is destined to endure in the spirit of Pitt, Peel, and Gladstone; and it certainly has not been an unmixed boon.

It is, I think, a signal error of judgment which led Mr. Gardiner finally to pronounce on "the failure of Cromwell's ideas." His institutions and his constructive schemes were undoubtedly recast. But his ideas — the best of his ideas — lived and developed. Mr. Gardiner himself seems to feel this when he says "that many, if not all, the experiments of the Commonwealth were but premature anticipations of the legislation of the nineteenth century." Surely, this is one of the strongest proofs of life, that ideas had borne fruit after two centuries. Mr. Firth states a precisely contrary view to Mr. Gardiner when he says: "The ideas which inspired Cromwell's policy exerted a lasting influence on the development of the English state. Thirty years after his death the religious liberty for which he fought was established by law." "No English ruler did more to shape the future of the land he governed." To ignore all this, as Mr. Gardiner does, is the nemesis of devoting a lifetime to the minute study of a single half century.

Let us turn to the wonderfully interesting and suggestive volume of Mr. John Morley. Its unique value consists in this, that Mr. Morley is the only one of the biographers of Cromwell who is himself a statesman and has served the State in critical affairs and responsible office. He is a man who has had to deal with some of the very problems that tried Oliver's mind — both ecclesiastical and temporal — parliamentary, educational, and Irish. The most philosophical historians have ever been men who have had practical experience of government, as were Thucydides, Tacitus, Machiavelli, Comines, Bacon, Clarendon, Gibbon, and Macaulay. We must now add the name of John

Morley to that of the statesmen historians, and his book to the list of the philosophical histories.

His volume has also another distinction, almost equally important, that of rare literary art, a distinction which he shares with Carlyle himself. It is full of subtle suggestions in political problems and of weighty pronouncements of political experience. It is this which distinguishes the book from that of Carlyle, to whom political experience was a sort of penal servitude, who solved every political problem with a Gargantuan trope or a resonant gibe. Mr. Morley's work is far wider in range than Mr. Carlyle's, who paints Cromwell as a being such as Cassius in sarcasm represented Julius:—

> "Why, man, he doth bestride the narrow world
> Like a Colossus; and we petty men
> Walk under his huge legs, and peep about
> To find ourselves dishonourable graves."

When Carlyle has to mention contemporary soldiers or politicians, they only walk under the huge legs of Oliver. To Mr. Morley they are all very real and active personages in the great drama. He gives us, as Clarendon did, a gallery of portraits of the men of the time.

This undoubtedly lessens the effect of the book viewed simply as a biography or portrait of Oliver. These speaking likenesses of warriors and politicians, this lucid unravelling of the conflicting forces in the great mêlée of the Civil Wars, somewhat disturb our contemplation of the presiding genius, and rather distract our attention from his directing influence and mastery. The book is entitled simply, *Oliver Cromwell*, but that is hardly accurate as a description. It is much more a history of the times wherein Oliver lived and worked than a biography of the man himself. Or rather, since five hundred pages cannot contain the *history* of such a half century, it is a series of brilliant appreciations of the typical events and men of the Civil Wars, Commonwealth, and Protectorate. In such chapters as II, III, and IV, Cromwell is very little on the stage, which is held by other actors of signal power and interest. We gain by having a great variety of scenes and a moving catalogue of *dramatis personæ*. But Cromwell loses by being presented amongst men who claim to be his equals and sometimes his superiors, and by not being at all consistently the hero of the piece. And this doubtless was to some extent Mr. Morley's own purpose and judgment. But perhaps the effect on the reader's mind may go farther than he designed.

I think we shall not be wrong in assuming Mr. Morley to estimate Cromwell, not only without any of Carlyle's unmixed adoration, but on a lower plane than Mr. Firth, and also perhaps Mr. Gardiner. Mr. Morley is enough of a philosopher to take a warm interest in Strafford, so much so that the drama opens with the great Minister playing some such part as Satan does in the opening of Paradise Lost. "He has as true a concern for order and the public service as Pym or Oliver," says Mr. Morley. Mr. Morley has a saving word for Laud, and will not allow that he was either the simpleton or the bigot that Macaulay pronounces him to be. But of all the men who figure in that great parliamentary crisis, Mr. Morley's favourite is — and most justly is — John Pym. In fact, a careless reader, who took up the book in haste, might think Pym was the leading spirit of the rebellion. And it is perhaps true that, in the matter of sympathy, Mr. Morley's heart goes out to Pym and not to Oliver.

As a loyal Cromwellian myself, I am not content with this estimate, which seems to me to carry the reaction against Carlyle's idolatry to unjust lengths. As Mr. Gardiner is inclined to minimise the permanent results of Cromwell's career by keeping his eye too closely fixed on the immediate future and the Restoration of Charles, so Mr. Morley is inclined to overemphasise Cromwell's unconstitutional policy, owing to his own excessive respect for Parliament and parliamentary methods. Mr. Gladstone once told me that he did not consider Cromwell so great a man as the late Lord Althorp, who was Mr. Gladstone's ideal of a successful leader of the House of Commons. Men whose lives are passed in the atmosphere of Parliament imbibe a superstitious reverence for oratorical battles and triumphs which often have little reference to the real history of the nation. And I cannot help fancying that Mr. Morley has caught something of Mr. Gladstone's disbelief in the greatness of a revolutionary dictator who was far from being a parliamentary success, but whose true greatness was that he lived in a higher plane than that of any Parliament.

The "prologue" to Mr. Morley's book (pp. 1–6) contains some of the finest passages that even Mr. Morley has added to English literature, and not a few of those Tacitean judgments on men and affairs which are his peculiar note. And in the "epilogue" (pp. 488–496) we have again more of these eloquent phrases and verdicts. I cannot wholly assent to all of these. The key-note of them is this: that Cromwell's essential claim to greatness is that of a soldier who won victories, that his political action was a series of mistakes, and that where force was useless he failed. Oliver, according to Mr. Morley, was the soldier of the great English Revolution, and not its chief. For my part I cannot quite accept all this, and Mr. Morley himself presently uses language that is hardly consistent. He speaks of "Oliver's largeness of aim; his freedom of spirit, and the energy that comes of a free spirit; the presence of a burning light in his mind; his good faith, his valour, his constancy," — these, he thinks, have stamped his name on the imagination of men over all the vast area of the civilised world. Precisely so, but these are not the qualities by which the mere soldier is remembered. As one who knew him said, "a larger soul hath seldom dwelt in a house of clay." It is this which so deeply impressed his contemporaries and made him the genius of the English Revolution.

It was not only this heroic nature, this largeness of mind, this burning light in his mind (expressions that we should not use of Wellington or Nelson) which raise Cromwell so far above the mere warrior, but it is his political genius and his resolute statesmanship that are his true glory. Perhaps the most marvellous part of his career is this, that, after all the fighting and confusion of the Civil Wars and the overthrow of Parliament and monarchy, England enjoyed for nearly ten years after Worcester, internal peace and order, without disturbance or revolution. To tell us that the man who secured this result, so marvellous when we consider what revolutions and civil wars mean, was not a statesman of commanding power, is surely a paradox. True, the institutions of the Protectorate perished in form, but not a few of them lived in spirit. As Mr. Gardiner says, these "experiments" were "anticipations of subsequent legislation." True, the great ideas of Oliver and his heroic experiments toward civil honesty and religious toleration were carried out one or two generations later by other men, and by parties who owed no allegiance to him. But that is the way with the slow evolution of social and religious reform. We might as well contend that Julius did not lay the foundations of the Roman Empire, nor Charles lay the foundations of mediæval Europe, nor William the Silent lay the foundations of Dutch independence. If Cromwell was a mere soldier, so were Julius, Charles, and Orange — who left nothing solid behind them.

Mr. Morley says very truly, "To ignore the Restoration is to misjudge the Rebellion." That is true enough if we narrow the Civil War and the Commonwealth down to a mere *rebellion*. But to ignore the deposition of the Stuarts and the resettlement of 1689 is to misjudge the English Revolution as a whole. And that is far more serious error than to misjudge the "Rebellion." The English Revolution which began in 1629 lasted at least for a century — as revolutions usually do. The Long Parliament, the Civil Wars, the Commonwealth, the Protectorate, the Restoration, the so-called "revolution" of 1689, the Hanoverian settlement, were all phases of it; but the Commonwealth and Protectorate were the decisive acts of it, without which the Long Parliament and the crowning mercies of Naseby and Worcester and the rest would have proved mere incidental rebellions. It is by fixing the eye too closely to the period from 1642 to 1662 that Mr. Morley, like Mr. Gardiner, somewhat loses sight of Cromwell's permanent work. If we look at the whole period, from the accession of Charles I to the time of Walpole, and regard it as one prolonged revolution, we may almost think Cromwell's share in the great evolution of English society was the only really dominant fact.

It is part of the same view that leads Mr. Morley to regard "Cromwell's revolution as the end of the mediæval, rather than the beginning of the modern era." If this be so, *cadit quæstio* — then Cromwell was nothing but a noble soldier. But here, again, one may ask : Was Julius's dictatorship the end of the republic, rather than the beginning of the empire? Was Charlemagne's reign the end of the barbaric invasions, or the beginning of feudal settlement? Was William's achievement the expulsion of the Spaniards from the Netherlands, or the beginning of Dutch independence? It is true that the Civil Wars and the Long Parliament ended the feudal régime in England. But Cromwell's entire bearing as general, as administrator, as protector, and as legislator, was essentially and utterly modern, inspired with modern ideas of honest law, social quality, capacity in lieu of birth, legality in lieu of privilege, religious freedom, and unlimited toleration for all serious opinions. Oliver, it is true, had little of the parliamentary leader, and nothing of the conventional democrat, but he was as much a man with modern ideas of progress as Walpole, Peel, or Gladstone.

In venturing to ask if Mr. Morley has quite done justice to my favourite hero, I speak with all the diffidence of a disciple who questions his master, and with a sense that this masterly portrait drawn by Mr. Morley accords in the main with that of Mr. Gardiner, who is far the greatest living authority on the period. It seems also to have satisfied another eminent historian, Dr. T. Hodgkin, who in the fifth, or February, number of the *Monthly Review* (p. 82), has published a sympathetic notice of Mr. Morley's book. Dr. Hodgkin incidentally takes up a point whereon Mr. Gardiner has condemned the judgment of Cromwell, in allying himself with France rather than Spain. Mr. Morley would seem to follow Gardiner in regarding the alliance with Mazarin as short-sighted policy in an English statesman. Dr. Hodgkin points out that the contemporary judgment of European diplomatists, and even of the acute delegates of Venice, was that the vast power of Spain was a greater menace to European peace and freedom than was that of France. Forty years later France was preponderant. But, as Dr. Hodgkin truly says, and Mr. Firth agrees with him, a practical statesman, dealing with the facts of the hour, could hardly be expected to foresee so distant and speculative a result.

Mr. Charles Firth, of Balliol College, Oxford, is an authority on the Civil Wars only second to Mr. Gardiner. He prepared the *Life of Cromwell* and of so many of the leaders of that age for the *Dictionary of National Biography*, and his edition of the *Clarke Papers* and *Essays* for the Royal Historical Society are known to all students of the seventeenth century. His *Oliver Cromwell* (Putnam's Sons, 1900) is the view of the Protector which best satisfies me. It is a full and detailed narrative of Cromwell's entire career based on exhaustive research into all the original sources. It is more complete than Mr. Gardiner's *Oliver Cromwell* (4to, 1899) — the history not yet being completed — and it is more strictly a biography of Cromwell than is the wide-ranging work of Mr. Morley. I cannot withhold my conviction that Mr. Firth altogether judges Cromwell's true work more justly than either

Gardiner or Morley, whilst he agrees almost entirely with their estimate of Cromwell's character and genius.

Mr. Firth supports Gardiner and Morley in rejecting Carlyle's ideal of the divinely inspired hero; he agrees with them in regarding Oliver as a consummate soldier and a conscientious and lofty spirit. But Mr. Firth sees in him also the great statesman and the founder of much in our modern history. Both as soldier and as statesman, he says, Cromwell was greater than any Englishman of his time; and we must look to Cæsar or Napoleon for a parallel to such an union of high political and military ability in one man. Mr. Firth could hardly rate higher than does Mr. Morley Cromwell's marvellous power as a soldier, and this is the more interesting from Mr. Firth's intimate knowledge of the personnel and constitution of the Ironsides army. And he rightly insists on the cardinal point that Cromwell, a middle-aged civilian, created the instrument with which he achieved his victories, and "out of the military chaos which existed when the war began he organised the force which made Puritanism victorious."

But it is not as a mere soldier that Mr. Firth considers Cromwell. He rightly does justice to his power as a statesman, even as a constructive statesman who has left permanent results in our history. Mr. Firth enlarges on Oliver's social and political reforms with more fulness and sympathy than either Gardiner or Morley. In his seventeenth chapter Mr. Firth explains the eighty-two ordinances of 1653–1654, nearly all of which were confirmed by the Parliament of 1656. It is true that all the laws of the Protectorate were annulled at the Restoration; but they are nearly all now parts of our daily life. The relief of poor prisoners, the maintenance of highways, the reorganisation of the Treasury, the settlement of Ireland and of Scotland, the union of the three kingdoms, — these are some of the subjects of legislation. Surely, these are not mediæval, but modern, reforms, and testify to Cromwell's "faith in Progress," in which Mr. Morley holds him deficient. On three sets of ordinances Mr. Firth enlarges — reform of the law, reformation of manners, and reorganisation of the Church.

Cromwell in truth made heroic efforts for a sweeping reform of the law, both civil and criminal. He did this, not of his own motion, but by giving a free hand to Sir Matthew Hale and other eminent lawyers. The reform of Chancery was established in 1654–1656, and was the basis of subsequent reorganisation of that court. Cromwell's noble protest against the bloody code of the criminal law was not finally ratified until the nineteenth century. But the abolition of the feudal tenures and the mediæval land law was confirmed at the Restoration, and has never been set aside. Altogether the Commonwealth and the Protectorate form one of the most important epochs in the history of our law reform.

A very competent lawyer, Mr. F. A. Inderwick, K. C., has traced this step by step in his book, *The Interregnum* (1648–1660). As he shows, it was "the foundation to a great extent of our present system." The suppression of duelling, the establishment of a letter post, the consolidation of highway acts, acts against adultery and the forcible abduction of women, — are not of supreme importance, but at least they testify to the modern, not the mediæval, spirit of Cromwell's government. Other great reforms were the restoration of the English language to courts of justice and the suppression of the antiquated Norman jargon, the simplification of pleading, and the abolition of fees to judges and their officers. But the great object of all law reform was, as it has ever been, the Court of Chancery; and, in this perennial struggle between tradition and common sense, no effort has been more determined than that of the Protector.

The efforts made by Cromwell and his Parliament for the reformation of manners, against cruel sports, duelling, immorality, swearing, drunkenness, and gambling, may have exceeded the public opinion of that age, indeed, of our age. But it ill becomes us to say that they were wholly devoid of permanent effect in that they were swept away by a profligate Restoration, if the progress of civilisation has at length put an end to their worst excesses. The reorganisation of the Church lay at the heart of Oliver, and in dealing with this Augean stable, his good work was naturally destroyed when an obscene Monarchy recalled a persecuting Prelacy. His valiant efforts to protect Catholics, Quakers, and Jews from proscription needed centuries to be fulfilled in deeds. But, as Mr. Firth says: "Cromwell's ecclesiastical system passed away with its author, but no man exerted more influence on the religious development of England. Thanks to him, Nonconformity had time to take root and to grow so strong in England that the storm which followed the Restoration had no power to root it up."

Mr. Firth is not at all satisfied that Cromwell's foreign policy was wholly mistaken and abortive. He says, "It was in part a failure, but only in part." Of the three dominant ideas of that policy, — (1) to uphold the Protestant faith, (2) to extend English trade, (3) to prevent foreign intervention in England, — the first only was misconceived and without signal result, the other two objects were triumphantly successful. Cromwell, as Gardiner has shown us, misunderstood many things, and was far too sanguine of possible good, in the complicated imbroglio of European diplomacy. But Mr. Firth rightly does justice to the grandeur of his conception, and takes due account of the difficulties of the situation and the prejudices of the age and school in which he was reared. What English statesman from Cardinal Wolsey, Queen Elizabeth, down to Chatham, Pitt, Palmerston, and Gladstone, has not misunderstood the play of European forces, and failed in many of his cherished adventures?

Cromwell's colonial policy, Mr. Firth finds, was a greater success. He was "the first English ruler who systematically employed the power of the government to increase and extend the colonial possession of England." It was during the Protectorate that the nascent colonies were consolidated into what may be called the nucleus of the Empire. In spite of the disastrous attack on Hispaniola, the capture of Jamaica laid the foundation of the British West Indies, which was the most fruitful part of his external policy, and produced the most abiding results. Cromwell is certainly the first systematic founder of British Imperialism; and he is honoured or denounced as such by the two parties which approve or regret that growth of the United Kingdom. But it is hard to doubt that the man who, for the first time, held in so firm a hand the three kingdoms, and who laid the foundations of the Empire across the seas, left solid and permanent effects on the history of our country.

The "institutions" which Cromwell designed were undoubtedly swept away by that flooded sewer we call the "Restoration"; but Cromwell never intended them to be permanent. He knew perfectly well that they were a temporary stop-gap, designed to give an epoch of calm and recovery to the storm-tossed land. He made no attempt to found a dynasty, or to resettle the Constitution. He spoke of himself as a constable put in power to keep order, to stem the tide of anarchy, and prevent return of the Stuart monarchy. These things he achieved whilst his life lasted, and for two years after his death. His great ideas, which he had attempted to plant,—liberty of conscience, final breach with absolute monarchy and feudal aristocracy, union of the three kingdoms, mastery of the seas, extension of trade, legal reform, and a colonial empire, — were all made permanent bases of English policy by his successors within the next generation, or at most the next hundred years.

In a fine peroration Mr. Firth has summed up his estimate of this work : —

"So the Protector's institutions perished with him and his work ended in apparent failure. Yet he had achieved great things. Thanks to his sword, absolute monarchy failed to take root in English soil. Thanks to his sword, Great Britain emerged from the chaos of the Civil Wars one strong state instead of three separate and hostile communities. Nor were the results of his action entirely negative. The ideas which inspired his policy exerted a lasting influence on the development of the English state. Thirty years after his death the religious liberty for which he fought was established by law. The union with Scotland and Ireland, which the statesmen of the Restoration undid, the statesmen of the eighteenth century effected. The mastery of the seas he had desired to gain and the Greater Britain he had sought to build up became sober realities. Thus others perfected the work which he had designed and attempted. No English ruler did more to shape the future of the land he governed."

This I hold to be the real Cromwell — the truth about the work of the Protector. And it seems to me a paradox to call this work "negative," or to deny that he left a permanent reconstruction on the face of his country.

REPUBLICANISM AND DEMOCRACY

# Republicanism and Democracy

A LECTURE DELIVERED TO THE POLITICAL EDUCATION LEAGUE OF NEW YORK

SOCIETY is a living organism — an infinitely complex organic system of mutually correlated organs, indispensable to each other, and having really no independent life. Human nature is not a bundle of sticks or a sack of potatoes. It is a living body; and it can no more be truly separated into parts than a living man can be separated into a digestive apparatus and a nervous system.

Society is an organism, and it must be treated as a whole. The elements of society (*i.e.* of humanity) can be separated only in thought, not in fact. The State, the Church, Law, Public Opinion, Economics, Ethics, are subjects which we may reason about separately, and detach in the abstract. But for all purposes of concrete application we must consider them as depending one on each other.

Now the popular social and political schemes treat society piecemeal, in arbitrary sections. They study society in analytic groups, and then they begin to act as if these groups were separable factors. It is as though physicians and surgeons, after studying the physical organism, first as skeleton, then as nervous and digestive apparatus, then as a circulating system, were to begin to treat any one of them by itself, as if bone, heart, or brain could be treated by drugs or instruments apart from the rest of the body, and without reference to any reaction such treatment might cause elsewhere. The socialist, the communist, the coöperator, the democratic reformer, the land reformer, the suffrage reformer, the temperance or sex agitation, confine themselves to one definite element or capacity in human nature, and go for their own particular remedy without any regard for the rest of the social organism.

I can only deal with these great social problems from my own point of view. And I have been trained in the Positivist school on the principles of Auguste Comte. Now the Positivist scheme, true to its uniformly synthetic character, treats society organically. Every one of the institutions, methods, doctrines, it puts forward has to be viewed with reference to every other. It is an attempt to restore health to the body politic by a comprehensive treatment of the whole constitution, and not by applying local remedies to particular parts or organs. This proviso should prevent many objections which are made by hasty critics. They estimate the Positive synthesis, bit by bit, in the light of their own analytic notions, quite overlooking the truth that each institution and doctrine in any really synthetic scheme implies the rest. And underlying all is the institution of a strong and active public opinion, resting on an organised education, moral as well as intellectual, common to all, and modifying habits and all forces. Without this vigorous public opinion, all social and political schemes are little more than *nostrums*. Having this public opinion to moralise the whole social organism, the weaknesses of institutions may be corrected and supplemented. All institutions and political devices need this.

Try the effect of a right moral education in the world, before you seek to pull things to pieces by legal and practical revolutions. Thus, when we reject communism as the solution of the industrial problem, we propose as the basis of an industrial society a moral (not a material) socialism. That is to say, we propose to obtain the end by transforming opinions and habits, and not by violently revolutionising social institutions. But how are we to transform opinions and habits, the communist asks? By forming, we reply, a new public opinion, by a complete education, by an educating body, by a religion of duty.

But we also presuppose, as an antecedent condition of such public opinion, a transformed State, one in which the workman is guaranteed all that the State can give to improve his material condition without injuring the rest of the community; secondly, a real republic, that is, a State wherein the ultimate power rests with the body of the people. By republic we mean a commonwealth resting on the will and devoted to the interests of all citizens alike; having these three qualities — (1) repudiating all hereditary functions or privileges, (2) renouncing all class exclusions, (3) recognising no property in any public thing. A republic is a commonwealth where the whole common force is directed to the welfare of all citizens equally, as its *raison d'être*. This is the normal and only permanent form of the body politic in advanced civilised communities of free citizens.

This republican type is practically, but imperfectly and irregularly, realised in England. In form, but in little more than form, we retain a monarchy, which an acute and conservative observer described as the "theatric," or show part, of the British Constitution. The monarchy preserves certain traditional features of England, exerts a steady and uniform pressure to keep society in an organic form, and at times no doubt serves certain useful purposes. But we know that in all the larger things, and directly the nation is roused and has a will of its own, the throne becomes a mere symbol, without the smallest power even of retarding a definite policy.

The other obstacle to the republican type is the existence of a hereditary chamber, which under the growth of democracy in the Lower House is becoming perhaps more powerful as a resisting force than it has been for the last sixty years. An hereditary chamber is obviously irreconcilable with any republican principle; and when this chamber is, in the theory of the Constitution, the equal of the elected chamber, and under given conditions is able for a time to make its equality felt, it becomes a very serious source of disturbance and embarrassment. Still, since it is admitted that the resistance of the Upper House is a purely temporary one, that its action is dilatory only, that it has no originating power to force on the country any policy of its own; since it becomes a merely formal registering body whenever a conservative majority exists in the elective chamber; and since it can never under any circumstances interfere in anything touching finance and expenditure,—it must be taken that the House of Lords has an indirect and retarding effect on the body politic, but not a decisive or dominant effect. Both monarchy and House of Lords, from time to time, affect English political development for evil, especially the second; but neither of them separately, nor even both together, neutralise the principle that England is a republic, a democratic republic, modified by powerful aristocratic and monarchic institutions. The republican type is fully realised in the United States, in Switzerland, and practically in many of the smaller states of Europe, such as Greece, Norway, Holland, Denmark, even though all of these retain a ceremonial monarchy, and it is essentially but not completely realised in France. A typical republic implies the complete extinction of all hereditary institutions, of class manners, and of all privileged orders, or churches, and France retains all of these things, though in very vanishing form. The United States and Switzerland are as yet the only complete types of the pure republic; though many persons will think that the unscrupulous power of wealth in America, and the low inorganic condition of social life in Switzerland, present evils as bad as the aristocratic institutions of England, if not worse.

The Positive synthesis, to begin at the beginning, is hostile to every proposal for aggrandising the State, whether of the imperial or the communistic type. As it trusts the main influence in the moral and spiritual sphere to education, so it would commit the main work in the political sphere to public opinion. As in the moral world the problem is to organise education, so in the political sphere the main problem is to organise public opinion. If we could accomplish that, all the schemes for increasing the power of the State may be reduced to a minimum. Positivism has carefully considered the mode of organising public opinion, in the first place by providing for the people a common education of a high and complete sort; next, by greatly increasing the leisure of the people by reduced hours of labour and constant holidays; thirdly, by the regular institution and immense increase of workmen's clubs and meetings for political discussion; fourthly, by the wholly new institution of requiring public appointments to be submitted to the test of public approval; and lastly, by guaranteeing, as a social and religious institution, complete freedom of speech. With this, the form of government would become a thing of minor importance.

We are all so saturated with ideas of parliamentary government that we do not easily imagine any other as possible. Parliamentary government in England is quite a special national product, apparently innate in the British race, and indigenous in our own peculiar social type. I am not prepared to deny that it may continue for many generations to work under a revised form in Britain; but it seems quite unfit for France and most other countries of Europe, and to be rather a scandalous parody even in the United States. From the point of view of sociology and of human society, we could not regard what is an anomaly in the British island as a normal type. So that what we say as to parliamentary institutions may require some modification when applied to this country.

Comte proposed to retain (for the present) a Parliament elected by universal suffrage with complete control over the expenditure, but not directly charged with administrative functions. For the effective control over the executive government he would rely far more upon public opinion than on Parliament. And that is what we are now coming to do. Parliamentary government still retains a vast power over the imagination and even over the affections of Englishmen, because it really represents to us the republic; it represents the People and Progress in the great struggle with Monarchy and Feudalism. To us, Parliament is the only instrument whereby a despotic executive has been curbed and shorn of its intolerance. Its glory is that it has been the moderating and humanising force of our monarchy. But now that the monarchy is a shadow, and Parliament has no function as a counterpoise, and the two Houses of

Parliament are now balanced in such a way as to produce a chronic deadlock, men are seriously asking themselves if Parliament deserves this regard and affection. What is there to show to-day that Parliament is the normal executive organ for an advanced republic? Do we see it to be so in the United States, or in France? On the contrary, in the only great and complete republics we have seen for the last two generations, the tendency of Parliament elected by universal suffrage is to make a stable and vigorous executive impossible, and that whilst failing to pass any sound system of industrial and social legislation. Like every other system devised and perfected to act as a check and a counterpoise on tyranny, parliaments are impotent in the ordinary course as positive organs of progressive government.

Parliamentary government is not truly republican except in great revolutionary crises, when it may become for a time a mighty engine of reform. The English Long Parliament of 1640, the English Convention of 1689, the first American Congress, the French States-General and Convention, our Reformed Parliament of 1832, did tremendous work of a revolutionary sort. But when Parliament settles into a mere institution, especially when it undertakes the administrative machinery of a vast aggregate of states, it soon ceases to be either truly republican, or really practical. In the first place, it passes largely into the hands of the rich, or of those who are seeking to become rich, or who are the creatures of the rich — as we see in England, in France, in the United States. Secondly, it passes under the control of the professional debaters, whether lawyers, journalists, or office-seekers, whose eloquence and activity is as little inspired by the welfare of the republic as that of an Old Bailey advocate is by the virtue of his client in the dock. Under the combined influence of the ambitious men of wealth, and of the professional men of the tongue, Parliaments too often sway backward and forward, doing nothing but debate and rearrange ministries, retarding, obscuring, and falsifying public opinion.

Parliament, in our country within the last two centuries and particularly within the last two generations, has completely changed its original character and function without any definite change in the Constitution, or any formal authority for the change. We still call it the legislature; but it is much more of a huge executive committee than a legislature. It passes new laws very slowly and occasionally; its financial business is settled in a few nights, often without any serious examination. But it devotes violent and prolonged debates to very small executive details, and brings the conduct of the State at last to something rather like government by public meeting. A common legal proceeding in Connemara or Shetland, the act of an official in British Columbia or on the banks of the Nyanza, are equally the subject for vehement debates. Is Parliament a consultative body, a ratifying body, or a law-making body — an initiative or a court of appeal? Is it a legislature, or is it an executive? It claims to be, and acts as if it were all of these at the same time and much more, as if it were kings, Lords, Commons, public meeting, High Court of Justice, international arbitrator, the grand official journal, and controller of all public officials, great and small, from a lord chancellor to a doorkeeper.

It is difficult to see how Parliament is to be at the same time a legislature and also an executive — for the body which controls, cross-examines, and modifies the executive, day by day, *is* the executive. The difficulty about a Parliament being the real Executive arises when Parliament is not homogeneous. In England at times the two Houses are in direct and systematic conflict. Then the plan is for the large minority in the Lower House, leagued with the conservative majority in the Upper House, to make legislation impossible and executive government as difficult as possible. Whilst the House of Lords remains untouched, that state of things is certain to continue; and it is difficult to see how popular legislation or a really democratic party can succeed, without some constitutional change. In the meantime, Parliament, divided against itself, is neither legislature nor executive in any active and free sense.

The legislative function of Parliament is not a reality, so long as nine-tenths of the hereditary House decline to attend, to listen, to consider, or to understand the points under debate, and yet have an equal voice in all legislation with the elected representatives of six millions. The executive functions of Parliament can only be exercised for harm, so long as every petty administrative act or order is liable to be debated by a miscellaneous crowd of 680 talkers, many of them ignorant, ill-informed, unscrupulous, and eager, not to do what is right, but to win credit for themselves and bring discredit on their rivals. Such is the ignoble end to which the mother of free Parliament seems too often to descend.

There is a great deal of solemn cant still pervading our superstitious reverence for parliamentary government. What does it mean? Parliamentary government means, literally, government by a talking assembly. But the real deliberative and critical assembly of the nation is a much larger and freer thing. It is the nation itself, quite as well informed of the facts as the M.P.'s, and meeting in ten thousand unofficial parliaments by day and night. The deliberative functions of Parliament are now quite superseded by public opinion; and the House of Commons is a very belated, imperfect, and often perverse representative of public opinion. It is easily converted into a retrograde and retarding force, as we often see in some scheme of social reform, which all parties in Parliament profess themselves anxious to pass, the principle and general lines of which have been heartily accepted by an overwhelming weight of public opinion, almost without any definite difference of purpose,— but which is still adjourned from year to year.

There is much more to be said for the doctrine of pure democracy — as now practised under the *referen-*

*dum* — the direct vote on a definite measure of the entire body of citizens. But a pure democracy of the Athenian type cannot be worked except in such a small community as that which met on the Pnyx, where the bulk of the active citizens in the state could all be assembled within the hearing of one man's voice. And the *referendum* — or direct vote — is only possible where the vote taken is a bare Yes, or No; the mere acceptance of a particular law, measure, or minister. No modification, qualification, or other variation is possible under any system of *referendum* or other type of direct democratic vote. Government cannot be carried on by crowds, or in crowds. A House of 680 members, coming and going, intriguing and grouping anew day by day, has some of the worst faults of a crowd.

The arguments for pure democratic government, for reaching directly the whole body of citizens, are all negative. They aim at getting rid of some evil; they do not pretend to claim any direct advantage. They appeal to the sentiments of jealousy, self-interest, and self-assertion. Their sole claim is to neutralise the effect of aristocratic or monarchic pressure. The most daring publicist has not ventured to assert that pure democracy, or the direct intervention of all in government, is *per se* the best method of obtaining efficient government. He only prefers it as a mode of preventing the people being forced to submit to what they hate, and plundered by those whom they cannot resist. The pure democratic principle was designed to combat gross abuses, ancient institutions, and rank superstitions. It has often served this end with striking success.

But the whole problem is transposed by the Positive scheme which would take from government its power for evil, and strengthen the people by a new organization of public opinion. Real republican sentiment is accomplished by this better than by any conceivable reform of the franchise or system of checks.

The first condition is a strict limitation of the sphere of government.

1. The chief and foremost limitation is to reduce the military function to pure defence. No one can pretend that this is possible at this hour. We are not here discussing what any President here, or any ministry in our country, are likely to do about the army and the navy. We are looking forward to a time when industry, not empire, shall be the end of human ambition and the desire of true patriotism. Standing armies might then be replaced by such an adequate militia, of which we already have types in the Swiss and the American republics. There, no doubt under very special geographical conditions, but conditions totally different, a free and proud people have organised a militia amply adequate to protect their independence, at a minimum drain on the freedom of the population, and a minimum of expenditure on the taxes of the country. At least this was true in the United States down to the war with Spain. Their scientific services, their staff, and in the case of Switzerland, their military organisation

N

and powers of mobilisation, are judged by experts to be ample for mere defence, and no other object can ever cross the mind of a Swiss. Wild as it sounds to-day, the day is at hand when Europe may abolish its huge armaments, renounce all military habits and prejudices; and having paid off their vast debts, the sinister inheritance from past wars, at one stroke reduce the national expenditure by one-third, or even one-half.

2. Next, of course, these vast aggregate empires must disappear. They are all the creation of war, they all exist only by chronic war, or preparation for war; and they all mean oppression and race tyranny. The Russian, Austrian, German, the British Empire, are all oppressive aggregates, with their origin in conquest, and their standing character of race ascendency. Nor are France, Italy, and Sweden without elements of the same kind in less marked degree. All of these vast tyrannous empires must dissolve before we reach a normal state, which will be that of smaller, homogeneous, industrial, and peaceful republics.

3. Without unnecessary armies and fleets, without scattered empires, and with no subject races to coerce, the sphere of the central govenment would be simple enough. It would be confined to maintaining order, providing for health, promoting and assisting industry in all its forms, and supplying a simple, cheap, and scientific system of law.

4. Lastly, the temporal government would have nothing whatever to do with any moral, intellectual, or

spiritual concern — neither with any church, sect, or creed; with no matter of education, with no academy or learned society. All these things would belong to independent, moral, intellectual, and religious movements. And this great end has been virtually attained in the United States — and only there.

Relieve government of its absorbing military duties; take it out of any class interest; remove from its sphere all religious questions, and suppose extinct all those vexed international questions, and incessant frontier wars in all parts of the globe, — and the sphere of government becomes simple enough and hardly a matter for desperate contention between rival parties.

The sphere of government would be reduced to this: — Protect the nation from foreign enemies; organise an efficient police; administer equal, cheap, speedy law; protect, assist, stimulate, and moderate industry; prevent groups encroaching on others; stop bands of marauders who seek to make aggression on other peoples, civilised or barbarous; provide for the health of great cities and of rural districts by establishing local bodies charged with providing air, open spaces, recreation grounds for the people, pure, unlimited, gratuitous water, which stands on the same footing as air, primary education, healthy comfortable homes for the people, museums, galleries, libraries, and other means of culture. These are the natural business of the local bodies; the task of the central government is to stimulate and control them, and arbitrate upon their mutual conflicts and rivalries. When government is reduced to these six great departments, when it is relieved from the care of vast armies and vast fleets, from the load of debt, from irritating questions of religion and education, from ecclesiastical patronage, from all direct care of education, from all hereditary pensions, from the absurd paraphernalia of courts, embassies, and sinecures, little would be left to struggle for. The national expenditure, even if doubled and trebled for public works, central museums, galleries, libraries, and so forth, might be reduced to one-third of our actual budget expenditure, which should easily be raised by a real land tax, a graduated income tax, increased succession duty, and customs and excise on luxuries only.

The furious struggles of our modern States, ranging from revolutionary anarchy to imperialist tyranny, rise out of the claim to determine a set of questions, all of which take their origin either in military or feudal habits. The ambition of Tzars and Emperors to dominate Europe, the ambition of our own imperialist parties to extend an empire scattered over the planet, create a tyranny, against which a desperate reaction sets in. Note the questions about which our rival parties have been struggling for the last ten years, indeed for twenty years; they may all be ultimately traced back to war, to thirst for domination, aggrandising the empire, securing the ascendency of some conquering race or order, or maintaining the privileges, and ascendency of some church or creed. Jingoism, the foreign wars in Asia and in Africa; Zulu, Ashantee, Matabele wars; Egyptian, Soudan wars; Burmese,

Afghan wars; Boer wars; the Irish struggle, the education struggle, the church struggle,—all have their origin in the effort of one race, or party, or sect, or order to domineer over others. When we rightly understand what is within, and what is not within, the sphere of normal government, and have forsworn war, class, and sect, the rage to wield political power will be found to be extinct.

We should then be no more consumed with the desire to direct the government of the nation than we now desire to determine in what part of the city shall be the beats of the A Division or the X Division of Police. The ordering of such matters of internal administrative will naturally pass into the hands of those who have special interest and experience of such details. The difficulty will be to induce capable citizens to concern themselves enough in such burdensome problems. With a sound system of public responsibility, entire freedom, organised clubs, the habit of complete publicity, the body of the people will exercise an ample general control. But, in the main, under the influence of a healthy education, they will be content with seeing that the work is well done, rather than insist on doing it themselves. If government were in a healthy state, and the people thoroughly educated intellectually and morally, if the sphere of government were strictly limited, and incapable of abuse by having no coercive power, we should as little hear of persons insisting on governing themselves as of making their own boots and shoes.

There is an enormous fallacy involved in the formulæ about people governing themselves. Strictly speaking, such a thing is impossible. It usually means that some govern the rest, usually one or very few govern certain groups, and then one out of several groups gains the ascendency for a time. Government means taking some one definite course out of a hundred. That one definite course in any complex case must originate in one directing mind, which impresses other leading minds, and these obtain the assent of more or less powerful groups, and ultimately one of these groups becomes strong enough to compel the more or less reluctant acquiescence of the rest. All government and all legislation, whether the government be that of a parliament, or of a tzar, or of a president elected by universal suffrage, means ultimately the will of some one, acquiesced in by overwhelming numbers. The despotism of the Tzar or the Sultan means that the decision of a ruler invested with divine right is supported by the superstitious reverence of a body of people strong enough and organised well enough to sweep down any opposition, the millions paying imperial taxes, and submitting to enter the imperial army without a murmur. The government of a parliamentary party means that what the prime minister thinks it wise and feasible to do, he induces his ministry to accept, and after a great deal of talk and compromise, the Parliament assents to the measures, or Lord Rosebery retires and Lord Salisbury carries his bills. That is much the same with President McKinley in the United States or M. Loubet in the French Republic. There is no essential difference between all five cases. The people govern themselves strictly neither in America, France, nor England, any more than Russia or Turkey. Ancient superstition in Russia and Turkey produce a more absolute and imposing authority for the time. Lord Rosebery and Lord Salisbury are liable to be checked and put out of office by Parliament or a general election. Tzars and Sultans are liable to be blown up by Nihilists or strangled by conspirators, and they have just as much trouble with students, ministers, and Ulemas as any prime minister with Parliament.

The future, we may be sure, will reduce the natural functions of Parliaments to those of inquiry, financial control, and legislation pure and simple, the elected Parliament meeting for moderate sessions at regular intervals, and having withdrawn from it administrative work, the supervision of ministerial routine, and any power to overthrow a ministry by a single vote. The presidential form of government, as recognised in the United States and partly in France, is a more natural type of government — the president being directly responsible to the body of the people, appointing his own ministers, without any limitation of his choice to members of Parliament, or parliamentary approval. It is a vain bugbear to raise a cry of dictatorship. It is simply efficient government with direct responsibility; the indirect responsibility to Parliament only tends to neutralise and falsify public opinion.

The Utopia of good government, then, would be, that, all hereditary and class institutions being eliminated, the sphere of government strictly limited, and a universal education being established, the people would be content to trust the temporal management of material interests to trained experts subject to those conditions: —

1. That the government have no great military force to compel obedience.

2. That their measures and appointments shall be submitted to ample public review before they are finally ratified.

3. That complete freedom of speech and criticism be a strict *sine qua non*.

4. That the budget be voted by a chamber elected by manhood suffrage.

5. That the government be directly responsible and removable by proper machinery, but not by a chance vote of a miscellaneous assembly.

The essential difference between the ideals propounded by Positivism and those of any despotic or any revolutionary school are these: The Positivist ideal would tend to reduce the authority of government whilst greatly enlarging the power of public opinion. The despotic and revolutionary schemes aim at getting into their own hands the whole existing force of governments, in order to set up institutions even more violent, arbitrary, and pitiless than those which exist. Positivism equally repudiates the tyranny of tzar, emperor, demagogue, or Nihilist. It is wholly neutral as between the Black Terror and the Red Terror. It protests equally against both in the name of humanity — past, present, and to come. It rejects the claim of Romanoffs, Bonapartes, Hohenzollerns, Bourbons, or Guelphs to crush society in the mill of divine right and supernatural revelation. Nor can it recognise any kindred right in revolutionists to enforce their own crudities and dogmas on humanity at large. It refuses to place the interests of Humanity, past, present, and to come, at the mercy of a majority of the male adults of any nation for the moment. The male adult voters in any country are always a minority of a minority in any population; and it is a mere metaphysical figment that they have any moral claim to recast society by a vote.

The interests of human society are those which humanity has created after about fifty thousand years of toil; the institutions which the genius, labours, and martyrdom of myriads of men and women have slowly built up; the interests of the living children and minors who are always a majority of the population, and the interests of the vaster majority of unborn children in the infinite ages to come. Positivism refuses to acquiesce in the resort to bayonets or police in any form (be the agents of State authority adorned with eagles or with caps of liberty), to impose on human life any kind of institutions by State authority. And it is so completely sincere in this refusal, that it would refuse with horror to have even its own programme or institutions imposed by State intervention.

The social evils of society do need a complete reorganisation, but by moral, religious, and intellectual agencies, and on these the physical force revolutionists have even less to offer us than the reactionists. We do most assuredly need a higher code of duty, more social and less selfish habits, a deeper and more moral education. But it is no more in the power of a terrorist than of a despot to decree virtue and good citizenship. The Positivist ideal of the republic is one in which these — the main ends of social life — are attained by moral means, by religious training, by education, by an intensely active social opinion. The main work of Positivism, the main instrument of humanity in the future, is education, in the highest and widest sense of the term. The State, or material system of external order, is merely the condition, the preliminary ground, for this education. The State has to defend, protect, sanitate, and beautify the conditions of civic life. It must keep order, promote health, comfort, enjoyment, good citizenship, by suppressing nuisances and all overgrown or anti-social forces, to prevent citizens or groups from encroaching on the free life of other citizens.

A truly industrial, peaceful, cultured, and free life cannot be imposed by any kind of armed force or arbitrary law. These institutions must grow, spontaneously and normally. The republic, reduced to a manageable size and population, freed from all warlike ambition and from all fear of attack from its neighbours, will have little to do but to allow the moral and intellectual life of its citizens to develop in a healthy way, to prevent the encroachment of any on the lives and labours of others, and to furnish forth the material life of all with adequate means. The citizens will not want to burn down capitals, to blow up public buildings, to have a revolution once every ten years, in order to secure these ends. They will be willing to intrust power to really capable hands, watching, supervising, the way in which these functions are performed, discussing the way they are performed, making their own wants, complaints, and suggestions plainly heard, ready, if need be, to take the authorised modes of replacing these functionaries, — if they prove finally untrustworthy, — but not eternally correcting and embarrassing them, and not insisting on having every petty detail, whether of administration or legislation, voted on word by word in public and settled in furious party contests.

Such is the ideal of the republic — an ideal not applicable perhaps, hardly likely to be considered either to-day or to-morrow. For it is an ideal which assumes, as its antecedent condition, the existence of a living religion of humanity.

PERSONAL REMINISCENCES

# Personal Reminiscences

A LECTURE GIVEN AT THE WOMEN'S COLLEGE, BRYN MAWR, PENNSYLVANIA

I AM told by the distinguished president of this learned body that you would rather hear me talk about some of the famous men and women of Europe whom I have known, than listen to a set discourse on any general or historical subject. I am very willing to tell you what I remember; but I fear you can hardly be aware of the garrulity and egoism to which we seniors are prone, when invited to draw upon our memory of the past. Touching, as I do, on the term of life assigned by the Psalmist to the natural man, I can look back with a melancholy joy on the striking scenes I have witnessed and the eminent persons I have known. And it will be your fault if you tempt me to be guilty of a loquacity that may exhaust your patience. Remember, that in speaking of myself, I am acting only as a photographic plate, or a telephone instrument, to record impressions and to transmit words. And if I find anything to say that may be new to you, it is no merit or ingenuity of mine, but the simple accident that I was born in England in the reign of King William IV, whilst you have lived in America, at the end of the nineteenth century.

I was born, I say, under King William IV; and one of my early reminiscences is the coming home of my father from London with the news that "the King is dead." I was building a house of wooden bricks on the floor, and jumped up and asked — " Who is King now?" When I was told that there was no King, but that Victoria was Queen, I thought that a very poor end for a nation which had won the battle of Waterloo, and regretted that we had no Salic law in England. Do not laugh. Boys begin like that, as girls begin by thinking boys a mistake. But I was reconciled to a queen reigning over us, when I was taken up to London to see the Coronation.

I shall never forget that day, which remains on my memory more vividly perhaps than any day of my life. I was a child brought up quietly in the country, and it was my first experience of the vast city and the great world. Some of my family were in the Abbey, and I was placed in a window looking on Palace Yard, from which I could see the procession, the troops, and the crowds. I was deeply stirred by the masses of people, the equipages, the lines of soldiers, the force, the order, and the pageant of a great national ceremony. I remember Victoria in the bloom of her youth, and all the fascination of a girl queen entering on the rule of so mighty a kingdom. I eagerly watched the Duke of Wellington, the Marquis of Anglesey, who lost his leg at Waterloo, Marshal Soult who represented France, and Prince Esterhazy, who was the Austrian envoy. Nor can I forget the

Lord Mayor of London, in his painted and gilded coach, for he happened that year to be my own godfather. I remember questioning a huge life guardsman if he had killed many Frenchmen at Waterloo. (I rather jumped the interval of twenty-three years.) I inquired about the respective rank of the generals, courtiers, ministers, and judges, and could not decide whether I intended to be ultimately the successor of the Prime Minister or of the Lord Chancellor. That memorable day and its visions gave me my first definite interest in public affairs and the organisation of a State. I often think with gratitude on the good sense of my father who took the trouble to give such an opportunity of education to a child of six.

Later on, when I had come to live in London, of course I often saw the Queen, Prince Albert, and the royal family, the old Duke of Wellington, who would ride down Piccadilly in white duck trousers, tumbling about on his horse's back in a strange way, ever raising his hand to acknowledge the salutes of all who passed. I used to see Sir Robert Peel, Lord Palmerston, Lord Derby, and the ministers of their time, Disraeli, Napoleon III, the Tsar Nicholas, and the foreign royalties who came to our country. But as I never spoke to any of these exalted personages I need trouble you no longer with their names; and I will only say that they were all extremely like the portraits and engravings of them we know so well, and were even still more like the wonderful caricatures of them we may see in the old numbers of the London *Punch*.

o

I have taken you back for more than sixty years to remind you of all the enormous changes that have been introduced into the material side of life within my own lifetime. At my birth the locomotive had only just been invented, and the new police and cabs were on the first trial in London; but there were no railroads at all except in the northern corners of England, no ocean steamers, no telegraph but the semaphore, no cheap post, no electric light or other apparatus, and slaveholding existed in British colonies. You may think that life was not worth living under such conditions. I can assure you that life was quite as pleasant. You could walk in an hour from the heart of London into delicious meadows and woods, and we wrote a letter not oftener than twice in a week. But what will surprise you is, that our life sixty years ago was essentially quite the same as it is to-day, except that the pace was more deliberate and the leisure greater. We travelled abroad, read good books, enjoyed society, theatres, music, pictures, games, very much as you do now, though perhaps with somewhat less scrambling and elbowing of each other, and without any wish to be for ever "breaking the record" or our own hearts. And the moral that a septuagenarian might draw from the contrast is that we were quite as happy as you are, and not so very much inferior even as men and women.

But my business is to talk to you of the men and women whom I have known; and I cannot begin better than with one who was loved and admired in

America — I mean John Bright. I have heard some of his finest speeches, and to my mind, he was far the grandest orator of our time. The power of his oratory lay not in eloquence or splendour of diction, in the vulgar sense, but in the touching simplicity with which he went home to the right sense and generous sympathies of true men. When he welcomed William Lloyd Garrison on his visit to London in 1867, when he sprang to his feet in St. James' Hall to rebuke a member of Parliament who had insulted the Queen in a Reform meeting, when he described the silent ceremony of a Quaker's funeral, he impressed us with the religious solemnity of an apostle and with the pathos of poetry such as we feel in the lyrics of Burns or of Wordsworth. I was at times associated with him in committees, meetings, and social and political movements, where his sterling judgment and his manly spirit guided many a cause. And I had frequent opportunities of talking to him at clubs and social gatherings, where he was conspicuous for genial humour and keen insight. John Bright was hardly surpassed as a *causeur* in his time. He retained to the last the tone and manner of the simple provincial Quaker. I remember his taking me about the streets and squares of the West End one fine night in July, when we left a dinner party at Lord Houghton's, asking about all the great houses and crowded balls we passed with the amused curiosity of a country girl, and telling me a string of interesting anecdotes of his own youth and his own self-education in default of all academic training.

Richard Cobden I heard in one of the most striking examples of successful oratory that even he ever achieved. In 1857 Lord Palmerston suddenly dissolved Parliament and appealed to the nation to support him against the Peace party in one of his wanton wars on China. He challenged Cobden and his friends to hold a public meeting in London, which even then was entering on its career of what we now call Jingoism. Cobden, Roebuck, and Layard held an open meeting to protest against a policy of war. For a long time the meeting, packed with supporters of the government, drowned the voice of the speakers with interruptions and noise, and Mr. Cobden himself was received with an outburst of opposition. Time after time he waited, cool and smiling, for the storm to abate, but every sentence was cut short by violent tumults. At last he was able to finish a sentence or two of homely wisdom, and even to get a feeble cheer from a few friends. Again and again he was stopped and hooted; but at last he won over his hearers step by step. The cheers grew louder and more frequent; till at the end, he convinced the meeting of the justice of his cause, and he sat down amidst repeated volleys of hearty cheering.

I have often heard Gladstone both in Parliament and on the platform; but I doubt if he quite equalled Bright in majestic imagery as an orator, or, in convincing logic and unanswerable facts, quite equalled Richard Cobden. Gladstone, of course, was immensely superior to both of them in range of experience, in constructive power, and in the management of men. As I frequently met Mr. Gladstone in society, both in and out of office, and at times have stayed for days with him in a country house, I had abundant opportunity to observe his extraordinary versatility and the range of his reading, the rapidity with which he was wont to master intricate detail, his consummate command of every resource, and his beautiful courtesy of nature and considerate forbearance with all men.

If I were asked to pick out the three personal characteristics in which Mr. Gladstone surpassed all the eminent men of his time, I should choose the following out of his great union of diverse qualities. With a fiery spirit at bottom and a singularly masterful nature, he had a strange power of curbing himself at need and of keeping a cool head in the exuberance of his own oratory. Next, it was almost impossible to find any topic or incident into which he could not fling himself with interest and master it with rapidity. Lastly, of all men involved in a multitude of distracting cares, he had the most marvellous faculty of keeping his mind concentrated on the immediate point in hand.

I have seen him, when Prime Minister in arduous times, unbend his thoughts in easy society, so as to engage the first girl or child at hand in gossip about the most trivial things that occupied their lives. I remember the committee of a society of which he was Trustee calling him in to recommend a purchase they were proposing for acceptance to the body of the members. In twenty minutes, Mr. Gladstone mastered the details and the figures of the transaction quite as fully as the committee which had been studying them for three months. He left the committee room not quite convinced that the intended purchase was a good investment; but as the discussion went on in full meeting he completed his calculations and decided that it was. At length he rose, and opening with great deliberation, he stated all the points to be urged, both *pro* and *contra*, with extreme fairness, and left his hearers almost uncertain of his own bias. Gradually he warmed to the task, and seemed to be convincing himself whilst he convinced his audience, that the purchase would be good. He spoke for some time and ended by recommending the transaction with such energy that no doubt was left, and the proposal was carried. In the result, it has proved to be a great success.

I remember that in the house of one of his colleagues, when he was Prime Minister, I was thrust forward, somewhat unwisely by our host, to make an appeal to Mr. Gladstone on a public question, which was almost a kind of remonstrance. For a moment he turned round on me with the look of an old lion disturbed over a meal, as he not unnaturally resented what seemed an intrusion on my part. I showed him at once that I was entirely innocent of any presumptuous wish to volunteer my opinion, and was simply requested by his colleagues to inform him of a fact within my own knowledge that he ought to know. In an instant every sign of impatience had left him, and he invited me to speak of what I knew with the sweetest courtesy and kindness.

In the power of becoming absorbed in the matter before him, and excluding all outside interests for the time being, Mr. Gladstone had no rival in our age. He reminded us of the old stories how Archimedes solved an abstruse problem in his bath and then ran home shouting *Eureka*, quite forgetting to put on his clothes; how he was killed by the soldiers of Metellus whilst poring over his diagrams; or how Descartes, in abstruse meditation, walked into the lines of the enemy in war. Mr. Gladstone was certainly not an "absent-minded" statesman; but his power of abstracting his thoughts from all but the one matter in hand, greatly increased his energy, though it was often injurious to that all-round watchfulness which is essential to the minister charged with the complicated demands of a great empire. I have heard that in the midst of great political crises, when the existence of the party hung on some decision of the Cabinet, he would be absorbed in some new book on Homer, or church history, or the life of a college friend, until the hour of the meeting of council had actually struck.

We shall know all about Mr. Gladstone very soon (I hope within the year) when we have the *Life* by Mr. John Morley, for which the world has so long been looking with expectation. It is a fortunate conjunction of events that the biography of our illustrious statesman should have fallen into the hands of one of his colleagues, his close friend and confidant, who is at the same time one of the chiefs of English letters. No politician knew Mr. Gladstone's mind for the later part of his career so intimately as John Morley; no English writer could so fitly expound it to the world. What would we not have given if Milton had written a *Life* of Cromwell — or Swift that of Walpole — or Burke that of Pitt? The great writer and the great statesman do not often live in the same world; and when they do, they are seldom bound together with the same sympathies and kindred ideas.

As to Mr. John Morley himself, I am not going to tell you anything. He has been my close friend for some thirty-five years; and happily he has still, we trust, to add to his great record and to complete his career. Of living persons I shall not speak, for I might have to express some difference of opinion or to attribute to them something they would hasten to disclaim. There is no known rule such as *de vivis nil nisi bonum*. So anything that might occur to me to say as to such famous persons as Lord Rosebery and Sir William Harcourt, Mr. Morley and Mr. Chamberlain, will have to be remitted to my literary executors — if ever I were to become in my old age so garrulous and so silly as to presume to name literary executors at all.

I turn then to the illustrious thinkers and writers with whom I have been privileged to speak, — men and women whose names are household words in America as in Europe. Not that I shall presume to pass any judgment upon them or to weigh their influence, but simply to tell you in a few personal touches how they looked and seemed in the flesh to one who had the good fortune to be admitted to their presence. *Virgilium vidi tantum:* and I will try and tell you how he struck me.

I did not see Carlyle until he was an old man, after the death of his wife, living in retirement. A more dignified, courteous, and friendly senior it was impossible to imagine. He sate by his simple fireside, in the house in which he lived for forty-six years, and poured out *Latter-day Pamphlets* with great energy and strong Lowland accent. The effect was startling. He was exactly like all his portraits — the Whistler is the best both in art and in likeness — the words were strangely the same as he used in his fiercest hour, nay even exceeding this, for he wished that many people and things "might all be dawmed doun to hale" — so that it seemed an illusion, as if some wraith of Sartor had been summoned up to give a mocking presentation of the prophet. He said what he had so often said, till it seemed to me as if he were repeating thoughts which were graven in his memory. His bonhommie, his fire, his friendly manners struck me deeply. Once I called on him at the request of Madame Michelet to ask him to subscribe to the monument in Paris of Jules Michelet, which he willingly did, speaking of the historian with honour and friendship.

He was surprised to learn that I was a lawyer in practice. This he regretted, and he urged me to turn to letters, which did not seem to me very wise advice, as I had other interests and duties apart from letters or from law. For himself he told me cheerfully and quietly that his work was done, and he was waiting for the end, though at that time he was vigorous and able, with colour in his cheek and light in his eye. The last time I ever saw him was in the year of his death; he was still able to walk slowly near his house, but he groaned heavily over the burden of life, and longed to be at rest for ever with his kin in Annandale, strictly refusing a tomb in the Abbey.

The two Englishmen, who have held the widest European reputation, — Charles Darwin and Herbert Spencer, — are alike in this. Both reached extreme old age, though both, in a large part of their lives, were greatly hampered by very delicate health, permitting but a very restricted and intermittent study. As to the use of books, it is probable that few men of studious lives have spent so small a part of their time in actual reading. The right choice of books, the understanding of what they read, has done more for both of these thinkers than the midnight oil consumed over a library. It is genius, not omnivorous reading which makes the creative thinker. Darwin's conceptions, which have revolutionised the thought of the world, were based on what he saw, on reports of competent observers, but mainly on his own marvellous power of coördinating disparate facts in the natural world. I remember him as the most courteous, simple, and retiring of men, wholly unconscious, it would seem, of his own vast reputation, and of such painful delicacy of bodily frame and of such intense nervous sensitiveness, that he could not endure conversation even within his family circle for more than a limited time.

That Herbert Spencer should have produced his *Synthetic Philosophy*, and all his other works with the scanty time which his health has permitted him to give to books, is even more extraordinary than the case of Darwin, whose work lay largely in physical observation. Huxley once told me that of all men he had ever known, Spencer was supreme in the power to assimilate knowledge from the brains of competent students. I venture to assert that no thinker of his calibre has wasted so little time on mere reading, which should be a warning to those who fancy that learning can take the place of brains. Mr. Spencer's life for some fifty years has been a model of single-minded devotion to a great philosophic career. His resolute purpose to live his own life without hindrance from society, or distractions, or pursuit of fortune, fame, or rank; his unbending consistency and assertion of right and justice; his fervid enthusiasm for the cause of Peace, Industry, and Civilisation, form a spotless record in English letters.

Those who have known Mr. Spencer as a friend, as it has been my privilege to do, in spite of occasional literary combats and personal "difficulties," have reason to honour his stern independence of character and scrupulous equity, his noble simplicity of life, and his affectionate regard for the friends of a lifetime. The intellectual and moral sympathies that so long united Spencer, Lewes, and George Eliot were a singular advantage to all three, and are memorable in the records of English philosophy and literature. Three persons, with gifts and natures so widely different, lived together for many years in close intimacy and mutual respect. In looking back over the celebrities of the English world in the last half century, it is a pleasure to think that in Herbert Spencer we have still living the foremost philosopher of our time, a staunch apostle of humanity and the moral law which our age seems willing to forswear.

Thomas Huxley I used often to hear as a lecturer, to meet in society and at the debates of the Metaphysical Society. As a lecturer he was simply perfect: clear, incisive, illuminating, admirably adapting his words to the calibre of his audience. If he and I had sparring matches in the press or face to face, it was only an incident which I shared in common with others of every school and of any opinion. Huxley was a born controversialist,—" a first-class fighting man,"— whether the subject were science, theology, or metaphysics, and his skill as a debater has no doubt given a somewhat artificial rank to his purely scientific work. Personally, as his letters and the memoir by his son would show, he was a brilliant companion, and if the objects of his attacks were seldom delighted with his vivacity, his many friends and the bystanders greatly enjoyed it. He would fly at a Positivist with even more zest than at a bishop; nor did he always observe the rule laid down by Justice Stephen, one of his colleagues in the Metaphysical Society, that "dog should not bite dog!" Huxley was always ready to go for mastiff, bulldog, or terrier. He was proud of having added the term Agnostic to the language of philosophy; and he never seemed to learn that no mere negative could be a title worthy of a serious philosopher.

I have spoken of John Stuart Mill at such length in published pieces that I will only now refer briefly to my own profound regard for his fine qualities and immense acquirements. No more just, patient, and generous soul ever adorned our public life. One had to be admitted to his intimacy and to association with him in the public movements, to which the whole of his later life was devoted, to know how warm a heart, what fire of enthusiasm lay covered up, like a volcano under snow, beneath the dry, formal, antiquated official which the world saw as Stuart Mill. I spent with him the last night I think he passed in England, but a week or two before his sudden death at Avignon. I have visited his grave in that most romantic of cemeteries beside the rushing Rhone and in sight of the huge palace of the mediæval Popes. And as I meditated on the strange vicissitudes of his career and the historic associations of his last resting-place, I was filled with regret that I could not have worked with him and under him in the new organ of Reform which in leaving England he had contemplated to found.

From philosophers I pass to poets. And *the poet* of the Victorian era was obviously Tennyson,—just as Homer was "the poet" to all Greeks. I have said so much of Tennyson, in a published work of mine which bears his name on its title page, that I shall only touch on a few reminiscences of his person. In person, I make bold to say, Alfred Tennyson was the most striking and original figure of the whole Victorian era, if not in the whole gallery of British literature. His noble stature, stately features, and unique mien, very much heightened by unconventional clothing, would have made him an object to stare at, if he ever appeared in any public place, which he very rarely did. I saw him not seldom at the Metaphysical Society, of which he was one of the founders, and also in his own beautiful house at Aldworth, for I had the good fortune to occupy a cottage on the Blackdown within a walk of his summer home.

When he was in the humour (which one must confess was not always) he was an admirable talker, full of good stories, his memories of old friends and striking incidents, quoting lines from the poets in Latin, Greek, Italian, and German. He was fond of reading his own poems, and I have heard him recite the "Charge of the Light Brigade," which he was asked to do for the benefit of the survivors. I can never forget the glorious roll of the Greek hexameters when I have heard him declaim passages from the Iliad, as he strolled about his beloved Down in its mantle of heather and fern. He once told me how he came to write those magical lines in the "Princess."

"Tears — idle tears — I know not what they mean."

He had been wandering alone, he said, among the ruins of Tintern Abbey, thinking of the monks and their solitary lives in the epoch of its foundation, and then, looking up across the Wye, he saw the harvesters, girls, men, and boys gathering in their crops in the fullness of life and merriment. And the contrast of the old world and the new filled him with emotion, so that the lines came to him as a spontaneous inspiration, as if he were simply recalling some familiar song that haunted his memory.

Robert Browning, for all his original genius and fine culture in literature, painting, and music, had less of the eccentric in him than almost any famous man of his time. A man of the world to his finger tips, who knew every one, went everywhere, and had seen everything, he might pass as a social lion, but not as a poet, or a genius. His animal spirits, his bonhommie, his curious versatility and experience, made him the autocrat of the London dinner table, of which he was never the tyrant — or the bore. Dear old Browning! how we all loved him; how we listened to his anecdotes; how we enjoyed his improvised "epitaphs in country churchyards," till we broke into shouts of laughter as we detected the amusing forgery. At home in the smoking room of a club, in a lady's literary tea-party, in a drawing-room concert, or in a river picnic, he might have passed for a retired diplomat, but for his buoyancy of mind and brilliancy of talk. His heart was as warm, his moral judgment as sound as his genius was original.

I have been present at the funeral in Westminster Abbey of Darwin, of Browning, of Tennyson, and of Gladstone. All were impressive and memorable occasions; but they differed in tone and in form. When Charles Darwin was laid hard by the dust of Newton, to the great majority of those present he was a great name but not a familiar person, and in very rare cases, a friend. And there was something a little incongruous in the readiness of the Church to chant its Requiem over the bones of Evolution. At the burial of Tennyson there was gathered together a great and representative company of his devoted admirers and of English thought. But in the simpler funeral of Robert Browning were to be seen hundreds of men and women whose eyes were dim with the feeling that they were parting with a dear friend and a delightful companion. The burial of Mr. Gladstone was at once a great national ceremony and a day of sincere mourning to all sorts and conditions of men. The Crown, the State, Parliament, and the public service were all fully represented with a ceremonious simplicity of outward show that was so truly in keeping with him they were carrying to his grave. The total absence of pageantry was as impressive as the religious office was pathetic. And to thousands within the Abbey as to tens of thousands without, it was a day of real mourning and of solemn thought.

Of John Ruskin I have written so many pieces that I will only add a few words of personal reminiscences. I knew him first, in the heyday of his youth and fame, forty years ago when he was living with his father and mother in their beautiful home at Denmark Hill near London. He had finished the best part of his art work, and was entering on his social and economic career in the Cornhill papers *Unto this Last*. I can never forget his high spirits, his enthusiasm, his startling paradoxes, and his beautiful deference to his aged father — the very model of the "canny," practical, punctilious Scot of the old school. "Pray, talk to John and teach him to respect Political Economy!" he would say — and then, "John, John, what nonsense ye're talking!" as John flew off on some Shelleian phantasy that the cautious senior could not follow. He was then teaching working-men to draw — and to think — in the college founded by Frederick Maurice, Tom Hughes, Kingsley, and William Morris. No more brilliant and lovable personality has ever given life to English letters.

From time to time I saw Ruskin again and had letters from him, — often wise, ingenious, affectionate, now and then angered by some utterance of mine which he condemned, and sometimes full of intense pathos and despair over the evil days on which he thought himself to have fallen. He goaded me in *Fors* and by private letters to reply to his attacks on Darwin, Mill, and Spencer, and at last I did so in the little piece I called *Past and Present*, in 1876. The last time that I saw him, not very long before his death, was in his lovely mountain home on Coniston Lake, with all the fire and passion of his soul burnt out, his look one of majestic decay, as of some venerable bard of a departed age; gentle, calm, simple, and surrounded with every grace that nature and love could give to his last days.

The *Life and Letters of George Eliot* by her husband, Mr. John Cross, sufficiently show the intimacy that I had the honour to retain with our great novelist for the last twenty years of her life. Of her, too, I have already spoken more than once in published pieces, and I can add nothing to all I have said of her noble qualities and vast acquirements, of her loyalty and goodness toward her many friends, of the singularly conscientious thoroughness with which she poured her whole life into every work she touched. Only her intimate friends knew the exhausting labour which she bestowed on her books, and the untiring patience with which she strove to answer every call made on her attention by friendship, or her own household, or any incident of her literary life. Everything she did was carefully planned and studiously worked out; and whether it was a letter, the visit of a friend, a foreign tour, or the plot of a novel, she put into it the best she had, and the utmost pains to make it perfect. Where she failed at all, I think, was in spontaneity, verve, and *abandon*. This extreme conscientiousness to do everything as well as she could do it gave a certain air of stiffness to her letters, made some of her books overcharged and *langweilig* (this is especially true of *Romola*), and it certainly ruined her poetry.

One of my most interesting reminiscences was a little dinner at her house, when Anthony Trollope and she compared notes on their respective ways of working. Trollope said that he sat down to his desk every morning early and wrote the given number of words every quarter of an hour by the clock. George Eliot groaned out that she sometimes spent days in poor health and low spirits without producing a line, and often tore up and rewrote a chapter over and over again. "Ah!" said Anthony, "for imaginative work like yours that is right and inevitable; but my stuff has to be made at a more business-like rate."

George Eliot's name reminds me of another great novelist, a friend of hers, the Russian Tourgénieff, to whom I was introduced by Professor Kovalevski. Tourgénieff's person was the grandest I ever remember to have seen in the flesh. With a head that recalled the Olympian Zeus, on an almost gigantic and stately frame, he looked more like an ancient hero than a mortal of our modern age. His simplicity, his courtly manners, his singular union of dignity and *naiveté*, charmed every one he addressed. I can recall with sad interest his pathetic picture of modern Russia, that ambiguous land, he said, halfway between Europe and Asia, yet belonging quite to neither, his blushing over the transports of the student girls who fell upon his neck, whilst the youths dragged his carriage through the streets after his lecture at the University, — "a lecture," he said humbly, "that was strictly confined to Russian literature without one word of politics." His conversation was of a piece with his fine manners and noble bearing, — simple, serious, instructive, and poetic. I visited him in his quiet apartment in the Rue de Madrid looking out over a pleasant garden; and he talked sadly for an hour of Russia, from which he had been so long an exile. And I cannot forget how he came in from Versailles once with a large brown-paper parcel, which he seemed to cherish with great care. I asked if we could relieve him of his burden. "*Ah non!*" said he, "*ce sont les souliers de ces Demoiselles.*" This poet of European fame was pleased to be the errand boy and light porter for the shoes of his friends' girls!

Another hero of European name I have seen under many aspects, — General Garibaldi. I met him in 1859 in the Romagna, when he was at the head of his volunteer army, going from town to town and from village to village to rouse the people to withstand the return of Pope and Austrians after the Treaty of Villafranca. As one passed through the Duchies and the Bolognese, one could tell at a glance if Garibaldi had been there or not. If not, in that September, all was stagnation. If he had been there, it was a people rising to arm itself. I saw him again in 1864 in his triumphal visit to London, when enormous crowds filled the streets to see him, and the excitement became so alarming to the government of Lord Palmerston, that they induced the general, by the agency of Lord Shaftesbury and Mr. Gladstone, to cut short his visit, and abruptly to withdraw to Caprera. Garibaldi and his friends were quite aware of the intrigues that led to his dismissal, — the true inner history of which was told in a pamphlet that was suppressed at the time, but which may one day be known. Some years later, I heard Garibaldi at a so-called Peace Congress at Geneva, and was personally presented to him at his hotel. To see him approach, to hear his voice, and take his hand seemed to me as if I were brought face to face with an apparition or a wraith. How could one forget the strange historic costume and red shirt, the sweetness of his expression and voice, the saint-like gentleness of his bearing, with its ineffable air of benevolence, as a widow woman in mourning fell on her knees and begged him to lay hands on her son and dedicate the boy to the country? And this the hero did quite simply and seriously, looking for all the world like a picture by Luini of "Suffer little children to come unto me!"

Mazzini lives in my memory as the most impressive personality with whom I have ever conversed. He was always the apostle, the fervid preacher of a cause that had become his religion and his creed. The unity of Italy was to him a new revelation, of which he was inspired to tell the glad tidings of great joy. And what eloquence, what a torrent of thought and feeling, what a sublime faith in his country and its future! Mazzini made one understand the influence of Savonarola,—or one ought rather to say of Giordano Bruno, "the awakener of the souls that are asleep." It was a great time in those sixties for the "*Giovane Italia.*" Would that the manhood of Italy were destined to show forth in accomplishment the dreams, the aspirations, and the sacrifices of the noble enthusiasts of the *Risorgimento*. *Nel tempo passato, era anche io Italianissimo : — ma adesso!*

I was taken one night by my dear old friend Louis Blanc — himself one of the kindest, most honest, most devoted of doctrinaire democrats — to sup at the house of Victor Hugo. Victor had little of the poet or the orator about him. You might have taken him for a stout weather-beaten sea captain, bluff in manner, imperative in tone and gesture, hearty with his own family, and somewhat impatient with outside people. He was treated with a deference that is hardly shown in private to princes of the blood; when he spoke, even in whispers to a political friend, the whole room was expected to maintain strict silence. "Il parle," — said Louis Blanc, though none of us, except Naquet, the Senator, were permitted to hear the words. A fervent admirer would come up, present, almost on his knees, a copy of the poet's *Année Terrible*, and beg the favour of the author's autograph. I cannot honestly say that, in the course of the evening, I heard one word that was interesting or characteristic drop from the lips on which France and Europe would hang in expectation. But such is the way sometimes with your great poet in the flesh. To me it was enough to have seen this rare genius of modern France. He might have been a great soldier or sailor, — might have won historic victories or commanded an expedition to the Pole.

One other famous Frenchman, who also now lies in

the Panthéon, I was privileged to know — Léon Gambetta — in my opinion far the greatest orator of the century, and one of her sons to whom France has been least grateful. For I count it amongst the calamities of French history that Hoche in the Revolution and Gambetta in our time were cut off in their prime. I can never forget the roar of indignation as he bounded from his seat, when I ventured to ask him if France could have prolonged the struggle with Germany after the surrender of Paris. I was in France during the obstinate battle against Macmahon and de Broglie that is known as the "Seize Mai," and I had abundant opportunity to learn the extraordinary energy, sagacity, and courage with which Gambetta commanded the campaign which saved the Republic and eventually forced the Marshal to accept the second alternative of the famous dilemma — *se soumettre ou se démettre.*

Nor can I ever forget that it was Gambetta who publicly proclaimed Auguste Comte as "the greatest thinker of the Nineteenth Century." I am now, I think, the only English Positivist who had personal knowledge of Comte. I hope one day to give some account of what I saw and heard. I was at once admitted, without introduction or appointment, to a long interview in the quiet apartments in Rue Monsieur-le-Prince which have been kept as a relic for forty-four years since the death of the philosopher. Of the build and energy of Thiers, Comte had the small stature and wonderful nerve-force that is peculiar to the men of the south. He received me a young Oxford student, as a pupil of Richard Congreve, with singular courtesy and frankness. He asked me what had been my studies, what was my mental attitude, what I knew of his system, and about what I wished him to speak. It was the period whilst he was still engaged on his second great work, the *Polity*, with his sketch of a Religion of Humanity, of which I knew nothing, for I had read little but Miss Martineau's condensed translation of the *Philosophy*. I told Comte that I adhered generally to the Christian faith in which I had been brought up; nor did he seek to disturb my beliefs. I stated in turn a variety of subjects on which I desired to hear his views. On each he spoke with entire freedom, clearness, and force. His oral exposition was far more easy to follow, and hence more fascinating, than his published books. As a lecturer his manner and resources were perfect. I left the philosopher profoundly impressed and greatly enlightened. From that day, I continued to study and meditate on doctrines which for forty years have guided my mind and my life, — in humble devotion to which I trust in Humanity to live and to die.

# MUNICIPAL GOVERNMENT

# Municipal Government

AN ADDRESS TO THE MUNICIPAL REFORM LEAGUE OF BOSTON

THERE has long been a tendency in Europe to regard Massachusetts and its capital city of Boston as the true intellectual, artistic, and religious centre of the United States. It is not for me to express any confident opinion on this delicate point; but as I am pretty sure that such is the rooted belief of all patriotic citizens of this ancient cradle of New England, I gladly accept the invitation of the Municipal Reform Union; and will say a few words on the subject of Municipal Organisation in general. It is a topic whereon I have long felt deep interest, which was much stimulated when I found myself unexpectedly coöpted as an Alderman of the London County Council in 1889. And I suppose that the problems of Municipal Organisation are precisely those whereon the citizens of the Republic have to meet the severest strictures, and whereon they may feel the most frequent misgivings.

I am certainly not about to repeat or expand any criticisms such as reach us in Europe of the weak side of American municipal institutions, least of all could I do so in Boston, where in things municipal, as in things educational and intellectual, so bright an example of progress and efficiency is presented to the whole Union. But as Mr. Bryce has told us, "the government of cities is the one conspicuous failure of the United States"; and the body of criticisms thereon which he has collected come from American and not from British sources. I am not about to repeat any of these criticisms, whether British or American; and I think it may be more useful if I tell you something of our own difficulties and failures, and the methods by which we have endeavoured to meet them.

I suppose there is not a single form of maladministration, bungling, jobbery, and corruption against which municipal reformers in the States have ever struggled, but what striking examples of the same evils have been rife in Great Britain at one time or other. The municipal government of London, Edinburgh, and Dublin a hundred years ago was choked with antiquated abuses. And it has been after a struggle, fought inch by inch all through the last century, that most of these abuses have been gradually reduced. Close corporations, hereditary franchises, bribery, sale of privileges, party nominations, have inflicted on our citizens ill-paved streets, public nuisances, incapable officials, secret favours, impure water, feeble lighting, and a burlesque police. All these abuses existed unchecked in Great Britain down to about seventy years ago, when the Reform movement began in earnest. British difficulties are mainly due to antiquity and conservatism — the ruinous legacy of old times and of class government. American abuses, I suppose, are largely due to youth, ignorance, inexperience, and the opportunities which unlimited democracy offers to an incessant immigration of refugees from Europe, unsettled, ignorant, heterogeneous, and necessitous.

In our country the conditions are reversed. Our emigrants largely exceed our immigrants. Our population is much more settled, and is organised in regularly defined classes and functions. The small area and dense population of our land affords a closer inspection and watchfulness of citizens over those institutions and arrangements which affect them. But the principal difference is this — that we have a considerable class of men, having wealth, experience, energy, and the habits of command, who are always ready to devote their time to the public service without reward or official rank. On the other hand in the Republic, the imperative sense of abstract equality, and unbounded faith in the electoral machine as the panacea and palladium of democracy, force men of wealth either to be idle or to stick to their counting-house, and force men of ability to disclaim any pretension to lead or direct their fellow-citizens except as their nominees and agents.

Take the case of London and mark the accumulation of difficulties, — physical, legal, historical, and social, — material and traditional obstacles to Municipal Organisation of a high type. The city itself is nearly two thousand years old, and still retains some of the geographical and geologic conditions that come down from the original Llyndyn, or the Hill in the Mud Swamp. Some of its streets are one or two thousand years old, dating from the Romans or the time when the city was restored by Alfred after the Danish destruction. Its Charter dates from the Conqueror in the eleventh century. Its corporation and officers date from the thirteenth century; and most of its institutions have several centuries of antiquity. The corporation has long historic and even constitutional relations with the Imperial Government and Crown. Its privileges and sanctities resemble those of the palace of Westminster or the Mace of the House of Commons. " Baubles " they may be, but to touch them sends a shudder through British respectable society. What with the complications of these venerable societies, to touch the *status quo* of London institutions is to assail the Ark of the Covenant. And then — what with coal smoke, foggy atmosphere, a muddy river, and a huge city with an area of thirty or forty miles in circumference — the obstacles to municipal reorganisation in London are somewhat formidable.

Prolonged and untiring efforts have at last done much to overcome these obstacles. The Municipal Corporations Act of 1835 made a clean sweep of the old obsolete monopolies, though it did not venture to touch the city of London which still remains a sort of Alsatia — or city of refuge for incorrigible survivals. The Metropolitan Board of Works was an attempt to unite the authorities of the Metropolis in one body; but its incompetence and jobbery led to its end in

1888. In 1889 the London County Council was established; and by common consent it has proved itself an immense improvement on the old Board of Works. It is truly representative of all classes of the kingdom, and at different times it has had as its elected members peers, statesmen, Cabinet Councillors, Members of Parliament, eminent servants of the Crown, lawyers, bankers, merchants, manufacturers, soldiers, artists, tradesmen, engineers, trades union officials, and working-men; and these classes have been represented by a wide and honest suffrage. The body is therefore peculiarly democratic in constitution, whilst long public service and youth, wealth, rank, and labour are mixed together in a degree hardly to be found in any other governing body in England, or perhaps one may add, in Europe.

This body, on which I had the honour of serving for some years, has certainly solved the problem of an elective municipal council being able to maintain a reputation for the strictest purity and the most rigid economy. Its offices have been filled by some of the most eminent statesmen, the most experienced public officials, and some of the most trusted financiers in the kingdom. Its first Chairman, Lord Rosebery, became the successor of Mr. Gladstone as Prime Minister; its budget has been framed by men who have spent their lives in guiding the financial and commercial interests of the Empire: and most of its departments have been served with an efficiency and economy which might do honour to any government. In the twelve years of its active career the County Council has not been accused by its bitterest critics — for, as an eminently democratic and reforming body, of course it has these — with the suspicion of jobbery, waste, or corruption in any of its members.

The whole of the services given by the members — even where they amount to very close application to administrative routine — are entirely voluntary. No member of the Council receives any salary or perquisite whatever, except the Deputy Chairman, who is in the position of General Manager. There are no allowances of any kind for any purpose. If the councillor at the end of a long day's work needs refreshment, he has to pay for it; and if the Chairman invites his colleagues to an entertainment, he has to bear the entire cost. I do not know of any institution at home or abroad, public or private, which is served on a volunteer system quite so rigid. I could tell you of hardworked business men and professional men, some having great affairs of their own, and some with small affairs, who devote, not their leisure hours, but a large part of their busy day to the service of their fellow-citizens. And I might instance a philanthropic manufacturer who, in middle life, closed his own works, and for twelve years has given every hour of his time, without fee or honour, to the incessant drudgery of departmental management, — labour which a bank clerk would think ill-paid by ten thousand dollars a year.

There have been immediate effects from this creation of a body of men representing all sides of English society, and bent on carrying on the work of the public with strict honesty and thorough efficiency. It is no doubt one of the results of our having a settled and organised society in England, where men of wealth and power are brought up in a certain tradition of being a governing class, that a democratic election sends to work side by side on the same benches, magnates, millionnaires, old officials and statesmen, men of culture, traders, and wage-earners alike. They have plunged into all the knotty problems of municipal organisation, — rehousing the poor, improvement of streets, sanitary inspection and legislation, the war against unjust weights and measures, against adulteration of food, the general regulations for city building, prohibition of excessive height of buildings and unsafe erections, the purifications of the sewers, the supply of water, gas, electricity, the control of tramcars, the management and extension of public parks, the care of a vast body of indigent lunatics, and the foundation of a system of technical education. It would be too much to pretend that all of these duties have been performed with equal success. But there has been no real breakdown, and not a breath of corrupt influence in any one of these departments; and in many of them the most conspicuous progress has been achieved.

One of the salient features of the London County Council is the close connection it has with the Imperial Legislature and Government. About one-fifth or one-sixth of the Council are usually members of the Legislature or retired Government officials of the higher rank. Every important act of the Council, be it a new street improvement, a scheme of water supply, or fresh powers for sanitary inspection, involves an appeal to the Legislature, and full consideration in legal form by committees of both Houses of Parliament. As these Acts of Parliament are passed only after strict criticism and inquiry, and as both Houses are in so close touch with the Council, ample publicity and judicial impartiality has to be given to every application made by the Council for fresh powers. There is no room in such a system for hole-and-corner Bills, "lobbying," or personal interests. Committees of the Imperial Parliament may be slow, stupid, obstructive, and narrow,— but they are not known to be venal, timid, or servile. And the Imperial Government rejoices in its powers of clipping the wings and probing the schemes of the Council, which is far too democratic and far too favourable to Labour to find much encouragement in a conservative government of the old school.

Not only is the London County Council severely scrutinised by the Imperial Government of administration,— never very willing to show it any favour,— not only is it bound hand and foot by legislative bonds, but it is at every point open to the appeal to judicial decision in respect of the least infringement of its legal powers. The poet asked that terrible home question — *Quid leges sine moribus?* What, indeed, is the good of passing laws if public opinion itself is corrupt? And we may say — *Quid leges sine tribunali-*

*bus?* What is the good of laws if courts of justice do not honestly carry them into execution? Now here is the strong point, the true pride of our British institutions. From that of the Lord Chief Justice to that of a stipendiary magistrate, every English court is bound to administer the law, swiftly, impartially, inexorably, without the smallest concern of wealth, rank, office, reputation, or influence. No judge of any kind is elected by anyone, nor has he anyone above him to give him orders, nor has he any term to his office, nor can he be removed, even by the Crown. An English judge is a Rhadamanthine being who is no respecter of persons, who deals out equal decisions, alike to all, — one to whom magnate, millionnaire, or "boss," are simply "the defendant," or the "prisoner at the bar."

The effect of this is that any person, however poor or humble, who fancies himself to be aggrieved by any act of the Council in excess of its legal powers, can immediately bring the issue to trial, and he knows very well that he will get ample redress if the law is on his side. The judge, whether he sit in a police court or in the Royal Courts of Justice, will not care a straw whether the Defendant before him can control fifty thousand electors or fifty million sterling. Any unconscious bias he may have will usually lead him to suspect the doings of democratic bodies and leaders. And thus, the smallest attempt at jobbery, oppression, or corruption, whether in the Council, or any of its members or servants, is liable to be summarily dealt with by tribunals which it is absolutely impossible to influence, to mislead, to terrify, or to buy. The London County Council I take to be more free from anything of the kind than perhaps any other institution in our country, and the key of the system is the inviolable independence of the judicial body.

I have spoken of the London Council of which I have knowledge from experience, but I have no reason to doubt that much the same tale could be told by members of the Councils in the cities of Manchester, Birmingham, Edinburgh, and Glasgow. In several points I believe they could point to success even greater than in London, partly because they are less involved in the maelstrom of Imperial Politics, and have not to contend against obsolete institutions, historic rivals, and a hostile government. The provincial municipalities of our country are for the most part efficient, popular, and entirely honest corporations, working under the three great conditions of good order that I have noted, — strong popular interest, trustworthy representatives, and an incorruptible and independent judiciary.

You may ask me if I have no reverse of the medal to show you, and if I mean to say that in London everything is for the best in the best of all possible cities. Far from it alas! Our great bane, as I am told it is yours in all municipal reform, is the curse of Party Politics. London is the seat of the Imperial Legislature and Government, and it is also the seat of our Imperial Finance and Trade. Ever since the democratising of our Parliament in the last generation, London has been one of the strongholds of the Conservative Party. Since its foundation twelve years ago, the London County Council, as an eminently progressive body, has been an object of jealousy and opposition to the conservative majority and government. And its efforts have been constantly thwarted by the Legislature and by the Ministry, when it has sought to free its citizens from monopolists of water, gas, and street traffic, when it has striven to tax the ground landlord, or to shake off the incubus of the antique privileges of the mediæval city.

We hear a good deal over our side of the water about your Tammanys and local rings, and as to the "Boss" system in American cities. Something of the kind is not unknown with us, under grander names and more sonorous forms. What is "Tammany," what is a "Boss"? You will correct me, but I am told the first is a close political caucus, a more or less secret society, pledged to vote in a body to keep up the material interests of its members and that of the classes and groups which it patronises and nurses. As a former mayor of a city, a very long way from Boston, told me, "the police of this town exist for the purpose of encouraging vice and of protecting crime." They say there are certain cities which are run by a sort of *mafia*, the business of which is to promote jobbery and to enable monopolists to thrive. Well! such things have been heard of in Europe, and one of the functions of our venerable House of Lords is to protect obsolete privileges to secure the material interests of its order and the classes it represents, and to prevent any interference with monopolies, exemptions, and antique claims that may conflict with the interest of the general public. And the business of the "boss," who in our country has a very grand name indeed, is by magniloquent speeches and lofty pretensions to see that the "ring" keeps its own counsel and votes the straight ticket in silence.

London, I believe, would have a model municipal government of its own were it not for three obstacles: first its physical difficulties, population, area, climate, ancient sites and encumbrances; secondly, the antique privileges and accumulation of legalised corporations within it; lastly the systematic opposition of a legislative House which is itself a typical monopoly and incubus. With all the differences between American and British municipalities, there are certain analogies and relations which make comparison useful and instructive. Both have their special difficulties to meet, their special advantages to use.

The cities of the United States begin with vast opportunities in that they are free from the three obstacles that hamper the complete reform of London. They start for the most part with a clean slate. They have not the physical obstacles to overcome, nor antiquated abuses, nor any hereditary legislature to wrestle with. The original cities of the Atlantic seaboard — Boston, New York, Philadelphia, or Baltimore — have had some trouble in dealing with the estuaries on which the old colonists placed them. But these troubles are nothing to the narrow streets and indestructible lines of Old London. Most American cities have an open area of boundless extent which, for such cities as Chicago, St. Louis, and San Francisco, attain to ideal conditions. The abuses of American cities are the creation of the last generation or two, and have not a rag of law or of sentiment wherewith to hide their deformities. And there is nothing hereditary in the United States,—not even misery, or vice, or crime.

But these advantages, I am assured, are neutralised, nay, more than neutralised, by other evils. I am not alluding to Boston, which I have every reason to believe is administered with a skill and an honesty that may compare with the most successful municipalities of Europe. But in other states than Massachusetts, I am told, the "ring" and the "boss" still flourish to the despair of the good citizen and the worrying of his life. Certainly, I have myself observed, in my travels through the States, eccentricities of paving, of building, of police mismanagement, public nuisances, which are more like Constantinople than this Republic. And when I ask how these things come to be endured by a people who pride themselves on being up-to-date in everything, if not indeed some way into futurity, I am told with groans that it is all owing to the "rings" and the "bosses," and the apathy of good citizens who have not the courage to face the "Camorrists," or are so much absorbed in their own private affairs that they have no time to give to the interests of the public.

They would have the courage to face the "Camorra," if every Judge in the United States were as free from any thought of fearing or favouring a "boss" or a "ring," as he would be of fearing or favouring a common pickpocket or a betting gang. And there would be plenty of competent men willing to give their time and service to the public, if the example of Boston and of the state of Massachusetts were more generally followed throughout the Union. Here we find a considerable class of citizens, quite satisfied with the fortunes they have inherited or made, who are ready to devote the rest of their lives to literature, science, and the conduct of public affairs. Hence have sprung all the Libraries, Athenæums, Colleges, Institutions, and Associations that delight the visitor in New England with their splendid endowments and admirable organisation. Splendid endowments are common enough throughout the States; but what is needed, especially in the newer states of the Republic, is a larger body of citizens of high culture and of spotless character who will show the way and direct their fellow-citizens in the path of reform.

The needs of the municipal reformer, I suppose, may be condensed in these two requirements: incorruptible judicial and legislative authorities; and secondly, the creation of a large class of men of culture and eminence, who will freely take the burden of public government in the sole interest of their fellow-citizens. The complete absence of all hereditary distinctions, the rule of abstract equality between all citizens, and the almost superstitious reverence of democratic doctrines make it no easy task for culture and superiority to gain a legitimate influence in the absence of great wealth or ambitious intrigue. But it has to be done if the "ring" and the "boss" are not to be perpetual institutions in the Republic; and though it takes time, it will be done in the end.

If a Reformer from the Old Country may give a word of encouragement and of caution to the Reformers of the New World, it is that they must make up their minds for a long pull, a strong pull, and a pull altogether. Municipal Reform is a very slow business, even slower than Parliamentary Reform or Political Reform. It has taken us in England the best part of a century; and we are not at all through our task even yet. Reformers must not be disheartened by the very gradual progress in their efforts. Progress often comes when it is least expected; for it depends very largely on waves of emotion unforeseen, and sudden revivals of conscience in the masses. Then again, the obstructives are all inspired by self-interest; and self-interests are continually coming to loggerheads amongst themselves. I will never suffer a doubt to cross my mind of the ultimate triumph of the Reformers; for their permanent failure to sweep away the municipal abuses of to-day would inflict a lasting wound on the welfare and the honour of the Republic itself.

# THE NINETEENTH CENTURY

# The Nineteenth Century

### An Address given to the Nineteenth Century Club of New York

WHEN I was honoured by an invitation to speak at a meeting of this famous Club, I felt very great doubt if I was at all adequately endowed or even justly entitled to do so. For I am opposed by conviction to what I am told is a first principle of the club, a debate of contrary opinions, and I am conscious of being curiously incapable myself of carrying on such a contest so as to afford the audience either profit or amusement.

Nothing, I think, is more idle and even mischievous than apodeictic debates in public, where no practical conclusions are possible or sought for, which end in mere talking parades, and where conviction is not desired nor sincerity of belief expected. I well remember the late Courtlandt Palmer consulting me in England when he contemplated the foundation of the Club on the basis of free (*i.e.* contradictory) discussion; and I gave him the historic advice given to those about to marry — "Don't!" The usual result of advice given of course followed, and the *logomachy* was started and has flourished. I differed from several of the views of Mr. Palmer, and in none more decidedly than in this. But when I received the invitation of the lady whom many years ago I had known in Europe, and who now takes so active a part in the literary and social life of New York, I resolved to do my best and trust to your good nature.

In all matters of freedom of thought I am heartily with you, and only doubt if freedom of speech is always the same thing. But as I am assured that this is a real Temple of Truth, and that sincerity of conviction is the motto of the Club, I will not venture on any of the current platitudes about the glories and progress of the Nineteenth Century, but I will frankly speak my whole mind, ai d come at once to the moral, religious, and social questions which underlie and are as important as railroads, telephones, and mammoth trusts. The new century on which we have just entered is a time for retrospection; and the least thoughtful of us can hardly help turning backward some passing thought about the Nineteenth Century which we have just laid to rest. I look back on it myself with a certain pathos as becomes my own time of life, as is natural to a veteran who remembers exactly two-thirds of the Nineteenth Century himself, and who doubts if its close fulfilled all the promise of its middle life. Not that I am a pessimist; but then I am no optimist. I am, as George Eliot said, a *meliorist*, who may believe that things are bad and may be even worse — but still are certain to be better one day.

I shall of course confine what I have to say to my own country and to Europe, and shall trust that the people of the United States have an easier record to look back on. In our own country I can remember the whole reign of Queen Victoria from 1837 to 1901, and can recall the coronation, the public festivals, the two Jubilee ceremonies, and the funeral in February last. My boyhood was passed in the stormy times of the Irish Famine, Chartist agitations, Free Trade struggles, Railroad manias, Bank panics, and the European revolutions of 1848–1849, 1850–1851. These were the days of Wellington, Peel, Russell, O'Connell Palmerston, Disraeli, and Derby, all of whom I often saw and heard, and followed with intense interest their political action. Wordsworth was the Poet Laureate, and Tennyson gave the promise of his splendid youth. Macaulay, Hallam, Grote, and Milman were the historians. Dickens, Thackeray, Bulwer, Kingsley, the Brontës were the romancists. Stuart Mill, Spencer, Carlyle, Ruskin were the prophets. Owen, Lyell, Faraday, Whewell were the men of science. Newman, Keble, Maurice, Martineau were the theologians. I doubt if we can show to-day a roll of equal power. I am certain that we cannot show to-day so high a tone of thought and feeling as that which inspired these men having gifts most dissimilar and beliefs so various.

But I pass from the memories of my early school and college days to the middle of the century, which coincided with my own entering on manhood. I cast my thoughts back to the hopes and ideas that were current in Europe when the first International Exhibition was opened in May, 1851, and men fondly thought that the world was entering on an era of peace, industry, and progress. The dream was broken by the *coup d'état* of Napoleon and the revival of the Empire; and soon followed the years of Crimean War, and then the Franco-Austrian War of 1859, and the Bismarckian wars of 1864–1866; and the great Civil War in the United States; and so on down to the great Franco-German War of 1870–1871. How truly melancholy it is to find ourselves forced by the tide of things to count epochs by wars, as if bloodshed and waste were the true landmarks in the progress of mankind. But wars and all they bring with them and all they leave behind them so colour the course of civilisation that they still remain the typical dates.

Now, my point is, that the generation counting from the abolition of Protection by Sir Robert Peel, down to the culmination of Bismarck when the German Empire was proclaimed in 1871, was an epoch of loftier ideals, more generous efforts, more robust intellects, healthier morality, and a saner philosophy than the generation which saw the close of the Nineteenth Century. The beginning of that generation saw such men as Wellington, Peel, Russell, Palmerston, Brougham, Cobden, Bright. The close of that generation was the epoch of Gladstone, Disraeli, Lord Derby, Lord Shaftesbury, Forster, and Mill. It was the era of the great movement for Free Trade,— which in our country, at least, was a social and moral reform that struck at a selfish and antiquated monopoly. It was the era of Parliamentary Reform and the removal of the abuses of a mere class representation of the people. It saw an immense reform in our system of taxation, which was made the most just and rational in the civilised world. It saw reform in the law: the emancipation of women from antique disabilities; the emancipation of workmen from oppressive laws and industrial serfdom. Finally, it saw the institution of a generous system of popular education. In Europe, it was the era of the overthrow of the effete tyrannies of mediæval and papal despotism, of the consolidation of Italy into a united nation, of the consolidation of Germany as a united nation. In France it saw the restoration of the Republic which has now lasted for more than thirty years. And in your country it saw the freedom of the Republic from the curse of slavery, the consolidation and the vast expansion of the commonwealth in area, in wealth, and in power. This age, I say, lived in a higher moral plane than does our age to-day. It was an epoch of humanitarian aspiration, not always wise, but with generous, moral, and social ideals before its eyes.

It has been my happiness to have listened to some of these moral and social ideals as they fell from the lips of those who led the thought of the Nineteenth Century. I had oral exposition of his system from Auguste Comte, whom Gambetta named as "the greatest thinker of the century." And for fifty years now I have diligently searched and reflected on his writings. The English philosopher, who in so many ways may be compared with Comte, and in so many ways must be contrasted with him, — Herbert Spencer, — I have known for forty years. In spite of some serious differences of opinion, I have never ceased profoundly to respect him, above all at this season, as the Englishman who has most emphatically condemned the recrudescence of the evil genius of war, conquest, and oppression of the weak by the strong. Nor can I ever forget the social inspiration that John Stuart Mill gave to his contemporaries, to such men as John Morley, and Leonard Courtney, Henry Fawcett, Sir Charles Dilke, and Auberon Herbert. To have listened to Carlyle, or Ruskin, or Mazzini, or George Eliot, as they descanted on their hopes of the future and their forebodings over the present, was to hear that which was at once a sermon and a poem. Tennyson, Browning, Hugo, and Matthew Arnold were our poets in those days, — men who at least "uttered nothing base," if some found them at times obscure or incoherent. To listen to John Bright on some great cause which touched his soul was to have a revelation of the just, stalwart, religious spirit of a Puritan of old. Will the Twentieth Century give us another Charles Darwin, — that immortal type of the man of science, inexhaustibly patient, preposterously modest, humble, retiring, and constitutionally careful never to go one step beyond his evidence? Will it give us another gentle, unassuming idealist like Tourgénieff, another historian compact of sympathy and imagination like Jules Michelet, another master of language like Renan, another orator and tribune of the Republic like Léon Gambetta? It was a liberal education to have spoken to these men face to face, to have heard their voice, to have watched the expression of their look as their thoughts rose to the lip.

Ever since the apotheosis of Bismarck in 1871, we have had in these latter thirty years imitation Bismarcks, wars of conquest and aggression, the policy of Blood and Iron, inflation of trade and of territory, "paying" wars, the enthronement of Imperialism. There have been wars in Europe, in Africa, in America, and even in the Pacific; wars in the Balkan, in Asia Minor, in Crete, in Greece, in Armenia, in Egypt, in the Soudan, in Abyssinia, in Tunis, in West Africa, and in East Africa, in Central Africa, and in South Africa; in Madagascar, in Tonquin, in Siam, in Burmah, in Northern India, in China, in Corea, in Cuba, in the Philippines. All of these have been begun, or continued, or have ended in domination, in a scramble for territory, ascendency, or loot. All have been needless, unjust, ultimately ruinous to the defeated and to the victors alike.

The people have caught the infection from their rulers, and are as thoroughly drunk with the lust of dominion as kings and ministers. Democracy has been discovered to be a more facile instrument of the "pirate boss" than aristocracy or monarchy itself. *Imperium et libertas* was the serio-comic motto of cynical Jingoism. It has proved to be merely one of the catchwords of the fraud. The real motto of this policy of Expansion is *Imperium et servitudo*. Empire spells slavery: moral, spiritual, economic, political subserviency. The connection of domination with servitude is as obvious as it is inevitable. To extend the rule of a nation over another race, be it barbarous or civilised, necessarily involves war; and if it be with an uncivilised people or a loosely organised people, it involves war usually in its most brutal form.

War, by its very nature, involves internal union and discipline, and *ipso facto* compels the suppression of all differences of view, the silencing of all criticism, and the postponement of all reforms. "So much the better," cry all obstructives and reactionaries — the bigots, the bullies, the privileged, and the monopolists. Some dreamy enthusiasts, like the crazy decadent hero in Tennyson's *Maud*, or the militant Boanerges of the churches have glorified these wars as schools of discipline, loyalty, and all the moral virtues. A war such as that led by Hoche, or Abraham Lincoln, or by de Wet may be all this. But a war of domination is a school of tyranny, injustice, and selfishness. Empire and war are such terrible ventures, so fraught with ruin and shame to those who fail, so disastrous to nations, and so full of horrors to the men and women of the defeated race, and not seldom to the conquerors as well, that when nations enter on them, they feel they must win or perish. They sacrifice everything rather than fail in their enterprise. If the cause is good, they are heroes; if the cause be bad, they become demons. And so they lie to themselves, they let men lie to them, they lie to one another, that their cause is good, knowing in their hearts that it is evil.

A nation given over to a wanton and unjust war — and all wars that are not in self-defence are unjust and wanton — is like a man given over to the madness of gaming. One throw more — be the issue misery or hell. They fling their very children to the wolves to speed the car of victory on its wild course. They mortgage their homes and their all to fill the bottomless pit of the war chest. Poetry dribbles down into a bloodthirsty doggerel — mere echoes of the weary catches they sound round the campfires in the veldt. Religion dribbles down into sanctimonious sermons on the holiness of war — one of the blessings, say the prelates of the Church, which the God of Mercy and the Prince of Peace vouchsafed to his creatures whom he made in his own image.

The infection extends to all forms of thought as well as to all forms of social progress. And as I contrast the last years of the century with its middle period, I find not progress but decadence. I indulge in no morbid Jeremiad nor in senile ill-humour with inevitable change. But, if it were my last word, I would insist that the close of the century has failed to fulfil the promise of its youth and of its prime. Forty or fifty years ago, the philosophy of Evolution, of Positive Science, of the new conception of Sociology, the vast world open to thought and to human life by the Reign of Law in the moral and social realm as in Nature and Physics — these conceptions filled the air as breathed by all solid and serious minds. To-day philosophy is stagnating in metaphysical maundering over "philosophic doubts," things which are verbal conundrums rather than thinkable realities. And Theology is evaporating in Christian Science, Theosophy, and the Mahatmas of some esoteric jargon.

I am not concerned to repeat the popular hymns to the scientific and material advancement of the Nineteenth Century, to the marvels of our mechanical inventions, to our colossal trade, wealth, industry, and energy. We all admit it; we all know it well, for it is dinned into our ears day and night by the brazen throats of a myriad-voiced press and the popular orators of our age. As the great orator of Athens said, "no need for long speeches to men who knew it all by heart." Not that I doubt, or dislike, or undervalue all this material progress. I am as heartily interested in it as the most up-to-date editor or the lightning leader-writer of the one-cent press. I am no obstructive, who desires a return to the Middle Ages or the narrow world of our grandfathers. Men of genius like Carlyle or Ruskin who do preach this only make us smile, and so far ruin the weight of all they say.

I am a modern, desirous to be up-to-date in all things, and heartily fond of all inventions, "notions," and appliances which do not tend to degrade our lives or drive us silly by their rattle or their pace. Let us give the able editor, the demagogue, and the syndicate promoter all he asks and all he boasts. There is another side to the picture of human life. And I make bold to say that, intellectually, spiritually, morally, socially, the close of the century, as contrasted with its prime, is to my eyes a picture blurred, darkened, and out of harmony and proportion. It is a fall from a higher plane, with its atrocities in South Africa, its desolation of two fine lands, its atrocities in China, in Cuba, in the Philippines, with its appalling famines in India, its infamies in Asia Minor, with its hideous slums in London, Paris, Berlin, New York, and Chicago, with its recrudescence of savagery, with its exploitation of the labourer, and its apotheosis of Capital.

And what is the cause of all this—what is the underlying perversion of mind and feeling that has set up this dry rot in our age? It is no one thing. It is a subtle, complex, conglomerate set of causes. In the first place, the apparent triumph of the policy of Blood and Iron in 1871, the visible gains won by Force, Ambition, and Selfishness. I am not speaking of the Franco-German War in any special sense; but of the Bismarckian policy as a whole. Bismarck presented to the admiring world the type of a practical and judicious Napoleon Bonaparte, who did not fail and ended, not in St. Helena, but with two hundred millions to his account, which his people laid out in very profitable investments. This novel combination of glory, heroism, and good business turned the heads of men in

Europe, from the British islands to the shores of Tonquin and Corea; and perhaps they find a modest echo on your side of the Atlantic as well.

Then came the enormous multiplication of mechanical contrivances and material advancement. But, whilst all this gave marvellous facilities to human life, it undoubtedly tended to vulgarise it, and stifled no small part of the poetry and romance of daily existence. The lovely country of Shakespeare became blackened with furnaces and pits. The roar of the railroads disturbed the peace of Gray's Elegy in a Churchyard and the serene meditations of Rydal Mount. And motors and tramcars invaded the quaint haunts sacred to the memory of Johnson, Goldsmith, and Lamb. Even the London of Pickwick and of Pendennis has vanished; and the modernised city, however magnificent and convenient, is not the soil which breeds more Pickwicks or Wellers. No one denies that the modernity of our daily life has given us vast facilities, but it somewhat tends to vulgarise it.

The marvellous diffusion of mechanical appliances for the use of science, whilst it has given us some astonishing means of observation, has tended to subdivide science into an infinite series of specialised and detached studies. The historian finds it necessary to limit himself to his two or three decades, or at most a century or two; the astronomer is either a strict nebulist or a confirmed lunist; the naturalist spends his life over the particular bug which bears his own honourable name. And so, the philosophy of the *Rerum natura* is relegated to popular manuals. *Synthesis*, or the theory which coördinates real knowledge, is mocked at as the vapouring of a crank. And the human value or usefulness of knowledge is thought to be vulgar curiosity. The enormous mass of accumulated facts, and their infinitesimal subdivisions have not only made their coördination next to impossible, but have made the idea of their coördination a dream like that of the "philosopher's stone."

Orthodox religion lost its creed, when its dogmas were found to be irrational and its history was proved to be fictitious. Its sacred books were discredited as substantial truth and were valued for their literary beauty and their sentimental charm. The result was that the moral system of orthodoxy was in conflict with the modern conscience. So the current theology took refuge in platitudes, in sentimental rhetoric about the loveliness of Jesus which nobody ever denied, and the "secret of Jesus," of which every one had his own interpretation. Having paid this homage to the Founder of their religion, the churches broke forth into hymns of triumph over the men who carried famine, bloodshed, ruin, and rape over the defenceless homes of innocent families in Africa and in Asia.

All this time not a word has come from our dominant Philosophy, or Science, or Religion to protest against the enormities which Christian powers have been perpetrating in China, enormities of which some cannot be described to the ears of women. The Nineteenth Century has left us a terrible legacy of problems — moral, intellectual political; international rivalries, industrial wars, metaphysical sophisms, cloudy theosophies, moral cancers. Can we of the Twentieth Century solve them? Will our electrical machines solve them, our telephones, our aerial telegraphs, and our X-rays? Will our wealth solve them? Or our numbers, our discoveries, our imitative wit? Will the waving of flags — whether with the three crosses or the forty-five stars — solve them, or will the shouting doggerel about Britannia or Columbia save us? Will our current Christianity save us? Why! the Churches, Episcopal, or Presbyterian, Baptist and Quakers have joined to bless the buccaneers; and our Christian armies, led by the favourite lieutenant of the most ostentatiously pious sovereign whom Europe has known since Louis XI, have committed atrocities in China, in the name of Christ, more abominable than those of the Crusades or the Inquisition. The lesson of the Nineteenth Century is that our morality, our philosophy, our religion have broken down. It is *Mene, Mene, Tekel, Upharsin* to our conventional morality, our nebulous philosophy, our hypocritical religion. Unless the Twentieth Century can recast morality, philosophy, and religion we shall go down a steep place into the sea like the herd of swine.

We need a social morality, an international morality, based on a genuine sense of altruism. We need a solid philosophy based on proof and leading up to the highest moral ideals of active life. We need a religion that shall have a creed as certain as geometry and the laws of physical science, and as wide and comprehensive as the human race. But, as I said before, I am no pessimist, but a real meliorist with unshaken confidence in a better time to come. The Nineteenth Century did not exhaust itself. It produced a new and systematic science of Sociology, the greatest advance of human thought since the Copernican and Cartesian renovation of science. That new science is instituted, however incomplete and however various its forms as yet. The systems of Comte, of Spencer, of Hegel may differ. But the conception of Sociology united them all. Sociology is the contribution of the Nineteenth Century to the philosophic evolution of Humanity; and no century since that of Aristotle has ever made a contribution of deeper import and of richer fruit. The Nineteenth Century too evolved the conception of Humanity, the greatest conception evolved since that of the unity of the Godhead; and with that came the underlying conception of the brotherhood of Man, the solidarity of classes, the greatest good of the greatest number.

The Nineteenth Century produced also a definite Religion — not a new religion — but the eternal imperishable Religion of Humanity, which existed in germ at the dawn of civilisation, which will be the strength and consolation of the Last Man in the Last Day of earth. I do not say this by way of limiting it to the special sense that Auguste Comte gave to that idea. I mean that religion of Humanity, which to-day is the secret hope and ideal at the bottom of our hearts and at the back of our brains. I mean that undefined but indestructible sense which is the religion of all good men and of all loving women, which some choose to call the ideal of Jesus — call it what you will — for the religion of Humanity incorporates, adapts, explains, and developes the inward spirit of the Gospel and the sermons of Paul. But it has this, which neither the Gospel of Confucius, nor of Buddha, nor of Jesus, nor of Luther, nor of Wesley ever had or pretended to have. That new characteristic which is peculiar to the religion of Humanity — which every superhuman theology cuts itself off from having — is a grasp of the whole field of human history; intense sympathy with every son and daughter of the human family, of whatever race, skin, or type; and above all, a trained knowledge of the vast results of science — the will and the wisdom to use this knowledge to the furtherance of a higher civilisation.